Mine Iwasaki

Biography

The Life And Legacy Of A Legendary Geisha

Mark Whittington

TABLE OF CONTENTS

CHAPTER 1
FLEETING MOMENTS OF JOY

CHAPTER 2
A WORLD FAR FROM HOME

CHAPTER 3
WEIGHT OF SUCCESSION

CHAPTER 4
GROWING INTO GRACE

CHAPTER 5
A SILENT GOODBYE

CHAPTER 6
SNOW

CHAPTER 7
A SYMPHONY OF TRADITIONS

CHAPTER 8
IN PURSUIT OF PERFECTION

CHAPTER 9
TOSHIO

CHAPTER 10
LESSONS OF THE HEART

CHAPTER 11
TRADITION MEETS MODERNITY

CHAPTER 12
PROMISES AND PRIDE

CHAPTER 13
SHATTERED LOVE

CHAPTER 14
A BOLD STEP TOWARD CHANGE

CHAPTER 15
THE STORY CONTINUES

CHAPTER 1
FLEETING MOMENTS OF JOY

Looking back on my life, I realize that the only time I was actually happy was while living with my parents. I felt safe and free, and despite my young age, I was left alone to do anything I wanted. After I left home at the age of five, I was never truly alone again, and I spent my entire life attempting to please others. All of my future joys and accomplishments were tinged with ambivalence and a dark, even tragic, counterpoint that became ingrained in me.

My parents were very much in love. They were an intriguing match. My father sprung from a line of ancient nobles and feudal lords who had fallen on hard times. My mother was born into a wealthy family of pirates who later became doctors. My father was tall and thin. He was quick-witted, energetic, and outgoing. He was also really strict. My mother was the opposite. She was small and fat, with a nice round face and large bosom. Where my father was harsh, my mother was gentle. However, they were both explainers, consolers, and peacemakers. His name was Shigezo Tanakaminamoto (Tanakaminamoto no Shigezo in classical Japanese language), and her name was Chie Akamatsu.1

Fujiwara no Kamatari, a guy who rose to the status of nobleman during his lifetime, established our lineage.

The Tanakaminamoto line has been around for fifty-two generations.

Historically, the Fujiwara family of aristocracy served as the Emperor's regent. During Emperor Saga's reign, Fujiwara no Motomi was promoted to daitoku (the highest rank of court minister established by Shotoku Taishi). He died in 782. His daughter, Princess Tanaka, married Emperor Saga and gave birth to Sumeru, the eighth prince in the imperial succession. As the emperor's retainer, he was granted the name Tanakaminamoto and rose to the status of independent nobleman.

Minamoto is a name that is still reserved for aristocracy nowadays. The family went on to hold other high-ranking positions, including court geomancer and shrine and temple administrator. For more than a thousand years, the Tanakaminamotos served the imperial order.

Japan experienced significant changes in the middle of the nineteenth century. The military dictatorship that had ruled the country for 650 years was deposed, and Emperor Meiji was appointed as the head of government. The feudal system was abolished, and Japan began to emerge as a modern nation-state. The emperor led a heated debate among nobles and intellectuals over the country's destiny.

My great-grandfather, Tanakaminamoto no Sukeyoshi, was similarly ready for a change. He was fed up with the aristocracy's never-ending factional infighting and wanted to be free of the onerous duties that came with his status. The emperor chose to relocate the imperial capital from Kyoto, where it had been for more than a millennium, to Tokyo. My family has deep roots in their home soil. My great-grandfather did not want to leave. As head of the family, he made the historic choice to relinquish his title and join the ranks of the common people.

The emperor pressured him to stay in the peerage, but he proudly declared himself a man of the people. The emperor insisted on retaining his name, and he complied. In everyday life, the family now goes by the shorter name Tanaka.

Despite his noble intentions, my great-grandfather's action had terrible consequences for the family's finances. Giving up his title, of course, meant forfeiting the property that came with it. The family's holdings stretched across thousands of acres in northeastern Kyoto, from Tanaka Shrine in the south to Ichijoji Temple in the north.

My great-grandfather and his descendants never recovered from their loss. They were never able to establish a foothold in the modern economy that was propelling the country, and instead lived in genteel poverty, living off their money and prospering on their antiquated feeling of intrinsic superiority. Some of them became highly skilled in the ceramic arts.

My mother is part of the Akamatsu family. Historically, they were famous pirates who plunder the trade channels surrounding the Inland Sea and out toward Korea and China. They amassed a sizable ill-gotten fortune, which they managed to convert into respectable wealth by the time my mother arrived. The Akamatsu family never served any Daimyo, although they had the power and property to rule Western Japan. Emperor Gotoba (1180-1239) gave the family the name Akamatsu.

While exploring other markets, the family learned a lot about medical herbs and their preparation. They started as healers and worked their way up to become house physicians for the Ikeda clan, Okayama's feudal barons. My mother inherited her ancestors' healing abilities and passed them on to my father.

My parents were both painters. My father attended art school and later worked as a professional painter of textiles for high-end kimonos and appraiser of exquisite porcelain.

My mother adored the kimono. One day, while visiting a kimono shop, she ran into my father, who immediately fell in love with her. He sought her relentlessly. My mother believed that their class inequalities made a relationship impossible. He asked her to marry him three times, but she declined. In the end, my father got her pregnant with my oldest sister. This pressed her hand, and they had to marry.

At the time, my father was extremely successful and wealthy. His designs sold for the greatest prices, and he earned a comfortable monthly income. But he was sending the majority of money to his parents, who had few other sources of income. My grandparents resided with their extended family in a massive house in the Tanaka district of town, which was staffed by a large number of servants. By the 1930s, the family had spent most of its savings. Some of the men had tried their hand as constables and government servants, but no one could keep a job for long. They had no history of working for a living. My father supported the entire household.

So, even though my father was not the oldest son, my grandparents demanded that he and my mother live with them after they married. Essentially, they needed the money.

It was an unhappy circumstance. My grandmother, Tamiko, was an overbearingly flamboyant personality who was dictatorial and short-tempered, the polar antithesis of my lovely, meek mother. My mother had been raised as a princess. But my grandmother handled her as if she were one of the helpers. She was abusive to her from the start, continually berating her for their shared heritage. There were some notable criminals in the Akamatsu family, and my grandmother acted as if my mother's line was polluted. She did not think my mother was suitable for her son.

Grandmother Tamiko's pastime was fencing, and she was an expert at using the naginata, or Japanese halberd. My grandma became enraged by my mother's stillness and began taunting her openly with the curved lance of her weapon. She would chase her around the house. It was odd and terrifying. One time, my grandmother went too far. She repeatedly cut through my mother's obi (kimono sash), separating it from her body. That was the last straw.

My parents already had three children at the time: two girls and one boy. The girls' names were Yaeko and Kikuko. Yaeko was ten, while Kikuko was eight. My father was in a predicament since he didn't have enough money to sustain both his parents and an independent household. He was discussing his problems with one of his business partners, a kimono fabric trader. He discussed the karyukai with my father and suggested that he at least try to speak with the owner of one of the establishments.

My father met with the owner of the geiko okiya, Iwasaki of Gion Kobu, one of Japan's top geiko houses, as well as one from Pontocho, another geiko neighborhood in Kyoto. My father secured places for Yaeko and Kikuko and received contract money for their apprenticeships. They would receive extensive training in classical arts, etiquette, and decorum, as well as complete support for their vocations. After becoming full-fledged geiko, they would become self-sufficient, with all debts eliminated and all earnings their own. The okiya would continue to receive a portion of their income as their career's agent and manager.

My father's choice dragged the family into an agreement with the karyukai that would have a long-term impact on all of our lives. My sisters were upset when they had to leave the safe haven of my grandparents' home. Yaeko never got over her sentiments of abandonment. She is still angry and spiteful to this day.

My parents and my elder brother moved to Yamashina, a Kyoto suburb. Over the years, my mother had eight more children. In 1939, they sent another of their daughters, my sister Kuniko, to work as an assistant to the proprietor of the Iwasaki okiya, despite their financial difficulties.

I was born in 1949, when my father was 53 and my mother was 44. I was the last of my parents' children, born on November 2nd, Scorpio in the Year of the Ox. My parents gave me the name Masako.

As far as I knew, our immediate family consisted of only eleven people. Seiichiro, Ryozo, Kozo, and Fumio were my four older brothers, while Yoshiko, Tomiko, and Yukiko were my three older sisters. I was unaware of the other three girls.

Our house was large and rambling. It was situated on the far side of a canal. The house was on a large plot of ground, with no other houses nearby. It was surrounded by trees and bamboo groves and backed up to a mountain. One accessed the house via a concrete footbridge across the canal. There was a pond in front of the house, surrounded by a stand of cosmos. Beyond that was a front yard with fig and pepper trees. Behind the house was a large backyard with a chicken coop, a carp-stocked fish pond, a kennel for our dog Koro, and my mother's vegetable garden.

The downstairs of the house included a parlor, an altar room, a living room, a dining room with a hearth, a kitchen, two backrooms, my father's studio, and a bathroom. There were two further rooms upstairs over the kitchen. The other kids slept upstairs. I slept with my folks downstairs.

I recall one incident with glee. It occurred during the rainy season. There was a large, round pond in front of our house. The hydrangea bush next to the pond was in full bloom, its vibrant blue complementing the green of the trees.

It was a completely still day. Suddenly, large drops of rain began to fall. I hastily retrieved my toys from under the pepper tree and dashed inside. I put my belongings on a shelf adjacent to the mahogany chest.

It began to pour shortly after everyone had returned home. The rain was coming down in buckets. In what seemed like minutes, the pond began to breach its borders, allowing water to spill into the house. We all raced around, taking up the tatami (straw matting). I found the whole thing quite humorous.

After we had saved all of the animals, we each received two pieces of strawberry candy with a picture of a strawberry on the wrapper. We were all rushing around the house, devouring sweets. A few tatami mats were floating in the water. My folks climbed on them and began using them as rafts to push themselves from room to room. They were having more fun than everybody else.

The next day, my father collected us and said, "Okay, everyone. We need to clean the house, both inside and outside. Seiichiro, take a crew and work on the back cliff; Ryozo, take a crew to the bamboo grove; Kozo, take a crew to clean the tatami; and Fumio, take your baby sister Masako and get directions from your mother. Understand? Go out there and do good work!"

"And what are you going to do, Dad?""Everyone wanted to know.

"Someone has to stay here and man the castle," he told me.

His battle cry fueled us, but there was one hitch. We had just eaten strawberry sweets the night before, and we were too hungry to sleep. We were famished. We had lost all of our food in the flood.

When we objected to my father, he replied, "An army cannot fight on an empty stomach." So you should go out and look for provisions. Bring them back to the castle and prepare for a siege!"

After receiving their orders, my older brothers and sisters walked outside and returned with rice and firewood. At the time, I was grateful for my brothers and sisters, as well as the rice ball I had been given to eat.

Everyone went home from school that day and slept like there was no tomorrow.

Another day, I went to feed the chickens and collect the eggs, as normal. The mother hen's name was Nikki. She became enraged and rushed me back inside the home, where she caught up to me and bit my leg. My father was upset and caught the hen.

He snatched her up and shouted, "I'm going to kill you for this." He wrung her neck and hung her dead body under the house's eaves. (Normally, he hanged them by their feet.) He kept her there until everyone returned from school.

When they saw her, they all thought, "Yum!" "We're having chicken-in-the-pot tonight," my father told them severely. "Take a close look at this and learn from it. This foolish beast bit our precious Masako. It eventually died as a result. Remember. Hurting or causing suffering to others is never acceptable. I will not allow it. Understand?" We all pretended we did.

That night, we ate chicken-in-a-pot made from the unfortunate Nikki. I could not eat it.

My father responded, "Masako, you must forgive Nikki." Mostly, she was a decent chicken. "You should eat so that Nikki can achieve Buddhahood."

"But, my stomach hurts. Instead, why don't you and Mommy assist Nikki to become Buddha?" I asked, offering a small prayer.

"That is a good idea. Let us all do as Masako asks and eat the chicken so that it can achieve Buddhahood."

Everyone prayed for the bird, dug in, and had a great time helping Nikki become a Buddha.

Another time, in a rare display of camaraderie, I was playing with everyone else. We climbed the mountain to the right of our house. We dug a large hole and dumped everything from the kitchen, including pots, pans, and dishes.

We were playing near my brother's secret fortress. We were having a terrific time when my older brother dared me to climb a nearby pine tree.

The branch broke, and I fell into the pond in front of our house. My father's studio fronted the pond. He heard the loud splash as I collapsed. He must have been astonished, yet he did not overreact.

This should have been the end, but my mother went into the kitchen to prepare dinner. Everything was gone. She called out to my father, who was bathing with me.

"Dear, I am afraid there is an issue. I will not be able to make dinner. What shall I do?"

"What on earth are you talking about? Why can't you cook dinner?"

Because there is nothing here. Everything we own has gone missing!"

I overheard this chat and decided I'd better alert everyone to her finding, so I started walking out the door. My father grabbed me by the collar and held me tightly.

Everyone quickly returned home. (It would have been preferable if they hadn't.) My father prepared to administer his traditional punishment, which involved lining them up and hitting each one over the head with a bamboo sword. I generally stood by his side (thinking, "I bet that hurts"). But not this time. That day, he roared at me, "You too, Masako." You're a part of this." I began whimpering as he lined me up with the others. I remember saying "Daddy," but he disregarded me and said, "This is also your doing." He didn't beat me as severely as he hit the others, but it was still a huge shock. He'd never hit me before.

We did not get any meals. My brothers and sisters sobbed while taking a bath. Then we were sent to sleep. My brother claimed that he was so hungry that he floated around the bathtub like a balloon.

My parents' interest in aesthetic pursuits resulted in a house full of beautiful objects: quartz crystals that glittered in the sun, fragrant pine and bamboo decorations that we hung up for the New Year, exotic-looking tools and implements my mother used to prepare herbal medicines, shiny musical instruments like my father's bamboo shakuhachi flute and my mother's one-stringed koto, and a collection of fine handcrafted ceramics. The residence also had its own bathtub, the old-fashioned variety that resembled a massive iron soup pot.

My father was the ruler of this small kingdom. He kept his studio at home, where he worked alongside a couple of his many apprentices. My father taught my mother the ancient Japanese tie-dyeing technique known as roketsuzome, and she eventually became a professional. My folks were known for their herbal cures. People kept coming over to ask them to make something for them.

My mother did not have a robust constitution. She had malaria, and it had weakened her heart. Nonetheless, she had the strength and perseverance to give birth to eleven children.

When I couldn't be with one of my parents, I preferred to be alone. I didn't even like playing with my sisters. I adored silence and couldn't take the noise that the other youngsters produced. When kids got home from school, I'd go hide or find another way to avoid them.

I spent a long time hiding. Japanese homes are modest and sparsely equipped by Western standards, yet they boast massive closets. That is because we keep numerous household items in them when they are not in use, such as bedding. When I was irritated or uncomfortable about something, or if I needed to concentrate or just relax, I would go into the closet.

My parents respected my desire to be alone and never forced me to play with the bigger kids. Of course, they kept an eye on me, but they always gave me my own space.

But I do remember lovely days when the entire family was together. My favorite of these were the gorgeous moonlit nights when my parents performed duets on the shakuhachi and the koto. We would crowd around to hear them play. I had no idea how soon these lovely interludes would cease.

But they soon did.

CHAPTER 2
A WORLD FAR FROM HOME

My father was planning a visit to Madame Oima and asked whether I wanted to join him. I loved going on outings with my father, so I agreed. My father informed me that we were merely going for a visit and that I could leave whenever I wished.

I was still terrified to walk over the footbridge in front of our house, so my father had to take me up and carry me. We strolled to the trolley and got onto the car going for Sanjo Keihan Station.

My universe at the time was still quite small. There were no other houses on our side of the bridge, so I had no playmates. So I was wide-eyed as I took in the views of the enormous city, the quantity of houses that lined Gion Kobu's streets, and the people who were present. It was exciting and a little scary. I was already on edge when we arrived.

The Iwasaki okiya, created in the beautiful architectural style of the Kyoto karyukai, was located on Shinbashi Street, three doors east of Hanamikoji. The building was long and narrow, with transom windows that faced the street. I thought it looked forbidding.

We walked through the genkan (entry vestibule) and into the reception area.

The venue was packed with women wearing informal kimonos. I felt odd. But Madame Oima greeted us with a bright smile. She was generous in her greetings and hospitality.

Tomiko appeared. She wore an extravagant hairstyle. To my surprise, she resembled a bride, particularly her hair.

Then a woman in Western clothes entered the room.

My father said, "Masako, this is your older sister."

"My name is Kuniko," she answered.

I was dumbfounded.

And who should stroll into the room but that extremely unpleasant woman, the one I couldn't tolerate, the mother of the boys who lived in our house?

I began tugging on the sleeve of my father's kimono, saying, "I want to go home." I couldn't take all of this stimulation.

When we got outside, tears began to fall slowly and steadily. I did not stop crying till we arrived at the Sanjo Keihan rail station. I recall seeing the elementary school with the turrets on top, so I know we were there.

We boarded the train home, and I retired to my usual solitude. My father appeared to grasp how I felt. He didn't try to talk to me about what had happened, but instead placed a consoling arm around my shoulder.

The moment we arrived home and saw my mother, I erupted into tears and pushed myself hysterically into her arms. After a time, I pulled myself from her lap and went into the closet.

My parents left me alone, and I spent the night submerged in the darkness.

The next day, I emerged from the closet, but I was still upset from my visit to the Iwasaki okiya. What I saw of the karyukai was so unlike all I knew. My tiny universe was starting to crumble. I was puzzled and afraid, and I spent most of my time embracing myself and staring into space.

About two weeks later, I resumed my normal routine. I finished my daily tasks and returned to "work." When I was too large to sit in my father's lap, he converted an orange crate into a desk for me and placed it next to him. I spent hours contentedly by his side.

Madame Oima decided to pay us a visit on that particular day. The sheer sight of her put me into a tailspin, and I was immediately back in the closet. This time, however, things were worse. I was so afraid of being outside that I wouldn't even go play under the pepper tree on the opposite side of the pond. I clung to my parents continuously and refused to leave their side.

Nonetheless, Madame Oima kept coming and asking for me.

This continued for several months. My father was worried about me and attempted to find a way to entice me back into the world.

He devised a scheme. One day, he told me, "I have a kimono delivery in town." Do you want to come with me?" He knew how much I enjoyed going out alone with him. I was still concerned about what might happen, but I agreed to go.

He led me to a kimono fabric shop on Muromachi Street. When we arrived at the door, the proprietor greeted my father with tremendous respect. My father informed me that he had some business to discuss and requested me to wait for him in the store.

The salesperson delighted me by showing me the various products for sale. The kimono and obi's variety and richness intrigued me. I could definitely tell, despite my age, that my father's kimono was the most gorgeous in the store.

I couldn't wait to tell my mother about what had happened, and when we came home, I couldn't stop talking about the kimono I'd seen. I went into a lengthy explanation for each one. My parents had never heard me speak for so long and were astounded by how much information I had retained. Of course, I'm talking about kimonos. I made a point of telling my mother how pleased I was that my father's kimono was the most beautiful in the store.

My father remarked, "Masako, I'm glad you liked the kimono so much. I have something I need to discuss with Madame Oima. Would you join me when I go to meet her? If we get there and you don't like it, we can turn around and head home. "I promise."

I was still mildly disturbed by the prospect of attending, but I have an almost obsessive need to conquer whatever scares me, and I believe this trait was present when I was three. I agreed to take the excursion.

We left soon after. I was quiet, but not as upset as the previous time. I didn't remember much about the house from my first visit, but the second time I went, I was relaxed enough to pay attention to my surroundings.

We entered the house through an old-fashioned genkan with a tamped earth floor rather than wood. The genkan opened immediately into a tatami room, or reception space. There was a magnificent screen at the back of this room that kept the inner rooms of the house hidden from view. There was a flower arrangement in front of the TV. A tall shoe cupboard stretched from floor to ceiling along the right side of the entranceway. Beyond that was a cupboard stocked with plates, braziers, chopsticks, and other kitchenware. There was an old-fashioned wooden ice box with ice blocks to keep it cool.

The genkan opened onto a corridor that stretched the length of the house, a long earthen passageway. On the right side, there was a scullery, replete with cook stoves. The rooms of the home were located to the left of the corridor.

The apartments were arranged one after the other, like a long train flat. The first room was a reception area or parlor. Beyond that was the dining room, where the geiko family sat to dine and relax. It had a rectangular brazier in the corner and a stairwell leading to the second story. The sliding doors to the dining room were open, displaying a stately living room with a massive standing altar. There was an enclosed garden outside the altar room.

Madame Oima invited us to the dining room. I spotted a young maiko. She was dressed casually and her face was unmade up, but she still had remnants of white makeup on her neck. We sat across from Madame Oima at the rectangular brazier. She sat with her back to the garden, and we guests were treated to the view. My father bent to pay his respects.

Madame Oima kept beaming at me while speaking with my father. "I'm pleased to report that Tomiko's classes are progressing well. She appears to have a natural ear and is learning to play the shamisen expertly. Her teachers and I are very happy with her progress."

I heard rustling in the earthen-floored corridor. I lowered my head to check and discovered a dog sleeping there.

"What is your name?""I asked him. The only answer I received was a bark.

"Oh," Madame Oima replied, "That's John."

"Big John would be a better name for him," I said.

"Well, in that case, I believe we should go ahead and call him Big John," Madame Oima replied.

Just then, another lady appeared. She was gorgeous, but she had a horrible expression on her face. Madame Oima called her Masako, which is the same as my name. But I gave her a nickname in my mind. I called her "Old Meanie". Madame Oima informed my father that this was the geiko who would be Tomiko's "older sister."

"I think the name John is fine," she remarked with a nasty voice.

"But Miss Masako thinks Big John is a better name," said Madame Oima, "and if Miss Masako here thinks that, then that is what we will call him." Everyone, please listen. From now on, I want you to call the dog Big John."

I recall this talk verbatim because I was so impressed by Madame Obama's strength. She possessed the ability to simply change a dog's name. Everyone had to listen to her and do what she said. Even Old Meanie.

I immediately connected with Big John. Madame Oima suggested that Tomiko and I take him for a walk. Tomiko explained where Big John came from. She claimed that some dog had an unlawful affair with a collie belonging to a well-known pickle manufacturer in the neighborhood, and Big John was the consequence.

Someone stopped us in the street.

"Who is that gorgeous little girl? Is she an Iwaaki?" the woman inquired.

"No, she's just my baby sister," Tomiko replied.

Then, a few minutes later, someone else said, "What a cute Iwasaki!My sister said, "No, she's just my baby sister."

This continued happening. My sister was getting quite annoyed. It made me uncomfortable, so I asked Tomiko if we could go back. Before she could respond, Big John turned on his own and began heading home.

Big John was an excellent dog. He was extremely clever and lived to the ancient age of eighteen. I always had the impression that he understood me.

We returned to the Iwasaki okiya, and I told my father, "Daddy, it's time to go home." I'm gone." I said a nice "bye" to everyone else before caressing Big John and bouncing out the door. My father said his formal goodbyes and followed me.

He grabbed my hand as we walked to the tram station. I didn't know what my father and Madame Oima were talking about while Tomiko and I were out, but I could sense he was concerned and disturbed. I began to suspect that something was very wrong.

As soon as we arrived home, I headed straight to the closet. I overheard my parents discussing. My father said, "You know, Chie, I really don't think I can do it. My mother replied, "I don't think I can bear to let her go either."

I began to spend more time in the closet, my peaceful womb amidst the chaos of family life.

My elder brother, Seiichiro, started working for the national railway in April. To commemorate his first payday, we had sukiyaki, and everyone gathered around the table to share the feast. My father made me get out of the closet and come to dinner.

Every night before we ate, my father would give a little speech. He would repeat the day's key events and congratulate us on our accomplishments, such as a school award or a birthday.

I was sitting on his lap when he congratulated my brother on his freedom.

"Today, your brother Seiichiro begins to contribute to household expenses. He's now a grownup. I hope the rest of you children can benefit from his wonderful example. When you become self-sufficient, I want you to think about other people and contribute to their well-being. Do you know what I'm saying?"

We said in unison, "Yes, we understand. Congratulations, Seiichiro!"

My father said, "Very good," and then began to eat. I couldn't reach the sukiyaki while sitting on my father's knee and asked, "Daddy, what about me?" "Oops, I forgot about Masako," he muttered, and began feeding me from the sukiyaki pot.

My folks were in a great mood. As I nibbled on one piece of meat after another, I began to reflect on how happy they were, and the more I pondered, the quieter I became and the less I wanted to eat.

I began to think. Is it preferable if I go to Iwasaki okiya? How was I going to accomplish it? How am I going to get there? I had to come up with a plan.

My favorite adventure was our annual cherry blossom viewing vacation, so I asked my folks, "Can we go see the cherry blossoms?" And then, can we go to the Iwasaki Okiya?"There was no logical connection." We always picnicked under the trees that bordered the canal's banks, which were just feet away from our front door. But I knew the cherry blossoms would never look the same from the opposite side of the canal.

My father answered instantly. "Chie, let's make a plan to see the cherry blossoms."

"It's a lovely idea," my mother replied. "I'll plan a picnic lunch."

"But after we look at the cherry blossoms, we may go to the Iwasaki okiya, correct?"

They understood how stubborn I was once I had an idea. My father attempted to divert me.

"I believe we should visit Miyako Odori after we see the cherry blossoms. Isn't that a better concept, Chie?"He asked my mother.

I intervened before she could respond.

"I'm heading to the Iwasaki okiya after we see the cherry blossoms. I am not going to visit Miyako Odori!"

"Masako, what are you saying?"I asked my father. "Why do you wish to travel to the Iwasaki okiya?"

"Because I want to go," I explained. "Then that lady will stop being rude to you and your mother. "I want to go right away."

"Hold on for a minute, Masako. The scenario involving that lady, Madame Oima, and us has nothing to do with you. You are too little to understand what is going on, but we owe Madame Oima a tremendous amount of appreciation. And your sister Tomiko has gone to the Iwasaki okiya to protect our honor. You do not need to worry about it. It is something that we adults must deal with on our own.

My father finally consented to allow me to spend one night at the Iwasaki okiya. I wanted to grab my favorite blanket and pillow. My mother gathered and packed them. I sat on the front steps, staring at the bridge.

It was time to leave. My mother came out to see us off. When we reached the bridge, my father went down to take me up and carry me as usual, but I said, "No, I'm going to do it myself."

This marked the beginning of my move to the Iwasaki okiya. It all started with that one night. A while later, I went for two nights. Then I began to visit for days at a time. The days turned into a month. Finally, a few months after I turned five, I moved in permanently.

CHAPTER 3
WEIGHT OF SUCCESSION

Auntie Oima was an excellent storyteller.

I spent many chilly winter nights cuddled with her near the brazier, toasting nuts and sipping tea. Alternatively, we may spend a sunny evening fanning ourselves on garden stools.

She explained how Gion Kobu came to be.

"In the past, there was an entertainment district near the Imperial Palace on Imadegawa Street near the river." It was known as the 'Willow World.' In the late sixteenth century, a great commander united the land. His name was Hideyoshi Toyotomi. Hideyoshi was quite rigorous and expected people to work hard. He relocated the Willow World away from the castle and out of the city entirely."

"Where has he put it?"

"He relocated it south to the town of Fushimi. However, people are naturally inclined to have fun, so a new sector of town formed to take its place.

"Guess where that was."

"Here?"

"Very good!" Pilgrims have been visiting Yasaka Shrine for thousands of years to see the famed cherry blossoms in the spring and maple leaves in the autumn. During the seventeenth century, pubs known as mizukake jaya arose near the shrine to serve refreshments to guests. These evolved into modern ochaya, and Gion Kobu sprang up around them."

Yasaka Shrine is located in the foothills of the Higashiyama Mountains, which form a chain along Kyoto's eastern boundary. The Gion Kobu, located west of the shrine, is approximately one square mile in size. The neighborhood is bisected by a tidy grid of maintained pathways. Hanamikoji (Cherry Blossom Viewing Path) passes across the district's heart from north to south, with Shinmonzen Street dividing it east to west. An historic canal carrying clean water from the eastern mountains flows diagonally through the area. The okiya was located on Shinbashi Street, which leads to the shrine's precincts.

Aunty Oima told me about herself.

"I was born here, shortly after Admiral Perry visited Japan. If Captain Morgan had seen me first, I bet he would have married me rather than Oyuki."

This caused us to roar with laughter. Oyuki was one of the most well-known geiko of all time. She had a patron named George Morgan, an American millionaire. He eventually married her, and they relocated to Paris, where she became a legend.

"No way were you as attractive as Oyuki!" We protested.

"I was more beautiful!" "Auntie Oima teased back. "Oyuki had a humorous appearance. She had a huge nose, but foreigners enjoy that kind of thing."

There was no way we could believe her.

"I started as a naikai and eventually became the head captain of Chimoto, a well-known restaurant south of Pontocho. I aspired to own my own establishment someday."

Naikai are the women in charge of organizing and serving feasts at ochaya and expensive restaurants. Being a naikai is a skilled job in and of itself.

"And I lived here, too," Aba added. "That happened before I married Uncle. We were one of the most popular establishments in Gion Kobu. You'd never seen such comings and goings. It was a great time."

"We had four geiko and two maiko," Auntie Oima explained. "One of our geiko was the brightest star in Gion Kobu. Her name was Yoneyu. She was one of the best geikos of them all. I hope you'll be like her.

"Mineko, Mother Sakaguchi's family had a large okiya back then. My mother, Yuki Iwasaki, was affiliated with them, therefore the Iwasaki okiya is a branch of the Sakaguchi okiya. That's why I usually consult Mother Sakaguchi for advice and refer to her as Mother, despite the fact that I'm ten years her senior!"

The story's elements gradually came together to form a logical whole.

You had a successful career. She was the highest-paid geiko in prewar Japan, guaranteeing that the Iwasaki okiya was one of the most prosperous houses.

She was a classic beauty, and men were all over her. One of her sponsors was a highly important Baron who paid her a large retainer. He provided her a stipend so she would be available to amuse him and his friends whenever he wanted.

This type of setup is not unusual. Having a primary geiko at your service is a significant status symbol in Japanese society. Gion Kobu saw great plenty during the 1930s. The region drew visitors from all over, including men from the top levels of the corporate sector and the aristocracy. They battled to support the most popular geiko. It's comparable to patronage at the opera, but instead of serving on the board, a man might choose to support his favorite diva. And, just as an opera patron does not anticipate sexual favors from the diva, the

Baron supported Yoneyu entirely on the basis of her musical perfection and the glitter she added to his reputation.

You got pregnant with Seisuke's child. On January 24, 1923, she gave birth to a baby girl at her okiya home. The family was overjoyed when they learned the news. A female child was a treasure. She could grow up in the okiya and, if talented, become a great geiko herself. She may even become an atotori. Boys, however, were a challenge. Okiya were exclusively for ladies. The mother of a boy child had to leave the okiya and live independently or give him up to foster care.

"What is Yoneyu's baby's name?"I asked.

"Her name was Masako," Auntie Oima said, winking.

"Do you mean Old Meanie?"" I was stunned when she first told me this section of the story.

Even though Auntie Oima did not have a daughter, I imagined Old Meanie was her granddaughter.

"Yes, Mineko, 'Old Meanie' is Yoneyu's daughter." She and I are not connected by blood."

When Masako was born, Auntie Oima, Yuki's natural daughter, was in line to inherit the business. She did not have any children of her own, so she adopted Yoneyu as her daughter to secure uninterrupted succession. Yoneyu was an excellent choice for a successor. She was knowledgeable about all of the accomplishments of a complete geiko and was able to train people who followed her. She had built up a big network of patrons to introduce to the geiko under her care, allowing her to sustain and expand the business.

One of the most important obligations of an okiya owner is to ensure an unbroken line of succession. Auntie Oima and You were looking for someone who could be next in line. They were overjoyed with

Masako's arrival. They prayed that she would possess the attributes and acquire the qualifications necessary for an atotori.

Masako began studying jiuta (a classical type of Japanese music and singing) at the age of three, and she showed remarkable potential. When she was six years old, she began taking tea ceremony, calligraphy, and koto (Japanese lute) classes. However, as she developed, it became clear that she has a tough personality. She was outspoken, sarcastic, and unfriendly.

Auntie Oima told me later that Masako suffered greatly as an illegitimate kid. Seisuke paid her regular visits throughout her childhood, but he was unable to openly recognize his paternity. She felt a tremendous deal of shame about this, and her humiliation exacerbated her naturally melancholy personality.

Auntie Oima and Yoneyu reluctantly concluded that Masako was not atotori material and would not make a decent geiko either. They advised her to marry and live the life of a typical housewife instead. As a result, when Masako graduated from high school, she was assigned to a temple finishing school to study wifely arts. But she despised it and returned home three days later. She resolved to stay at home until her elders found her a spouse.

I do not want to imply that a geiko cannot marry. Some of the most successful geikos I know were married and lived separately from their okiyas. I was particularly impressed by one geiko, a tall, willowy woman named Ren, for her ability to expertly manage the demands of an active career with those of a husband. However, most of us considered the prospect too scary and waited until we retired to marry. Others cherished their independence so much that they never relinquished it.

Masako was twenty years old when she became betrothed to Chojiro Kanai in 1943. He went to war. She stayed at home and worked on her trousseau. Unfortunately, the wedding never occurred. Chojiro was killed in action.

After they passed over Masako, the family had to find someone else to take Yoneyu's place. Auntie Oima was introduced to my father by a mutual acquaintance. Auntie Oima consented to bring Yaeko to the Iwasaki okiya. It was 1935. Yaeko was 10 years old.

Yaeko was a cute, outgoing, and humorous child. She was as stunning as the Mona Lisa. Auntie Oima and Yoneyu planned to train her to be an atotori.

Because of Yoneyu's immense success, they were able to make a significant investment in Yaeko's career, which they did. They introduced Yaeko as a maiko in 1938, when she was thirteen years old, under the name Yachiyo. Before the war, girls did not need to complete junior high school to become maiko. Some made their debut as early as age eight or nine. They spent three years preparing for Yaeko's amazing debut in the karyukai.

Decades later, people were still raving about Yaeko's magnificent outfit. They ordered Yaeko's kimono from the top boutiques in Kyoto, including Eriman. One of her ensembles, of which she had many, could have paid for a house. No money was spent in providing her with the finest hair ornaments and other maiko costume accessories. Auntie Oima often told me how extraordinary it was. She claimed that Yaeko's outfit was a direct reflection of the wealth and influence of the Iwasaki sponsors.

To commemorate the occasion, Yoneyu's Baron gave the thirteen-year-old Yaechiyo a ruby the size of a peach pit. It was hardly a lavish gift for Gion Kobu, where patrons are generous and costly gifts are the norm.

But Yaeko wasn't pleased. In truth, she was unhappy. She felt betrayed by my parents and resented having to work. She later told me she felt as if she had plummeted from heaven to hell.

Yaeko described her life with grandmother Tomiko as blissful. My grandmother adored her, and they were always together. Yaeko sat in her lap, ruling imperiously over her fifty-odd slaves and various family members. Occasionally, my grandma would rise up and yell, "Look at this, Yaeko!" and chase my mother with her lance. Apparently, Yaeko found this humorous.

Yaeko claims that when she was young, she had no idea that our mother and father were her parents. She assumed they were like members of my grandparents' staff and shouted out "Hey you" whenever she needed something.

So it came as a huge shock to her when she suddenly found herself living in the Iwasaki okiya, subjected to a stringent routine of teachings and ritual. She didn't realize that what had been heaven for her was misery for my mother. And, of course, she was too little to grasp their financial position. Her rage turned into a burning sense of victimization that she has carried throughout her life.

When Yaeko was sixteen, she fell in love with one of her customers, Seizo Uehara, a young man who frequently accompanied his father to Gion Kobu. The Ueharas were from Nara and owned a huge hat company. The connection appeared to improve her anger, and since Seizo was unmarried, it did not cause any problems.

Auntie Oima and You were initially satisfied with Yaeko's improvement. Yoneyu was the highest-ranking geiko in the Gion Kobu (and so throughout Japan), and Yaeko quickly rose to second place. Yoneyu and Yaechiyo became household names across the nation. The fortunes of the Iwasaki okiya appeared to be promising.

But there was an issue. It quickly became clear that Yaeko was not serious about her career. Frankly, a maiko, especially one as beautiful as Yaeko, can coast for a time on her wonderful outfits and youthful appeal, but her career will not flourish until she capitalizes on her talent. Yaeko felt sluggish and unmotivated. She became bored quickly and did not see things through. She despised lessons and paid little attention during rehearsals. Her dancing wasn't improving. Auntie Oima said it was making her very nervous.

They had invested so much in Yaeko, and now they were losing faith in her as the right successor. But You believed she had no choice. Masako was out of the running.

So, almost by default, she welcomed Yaeko into the family.

Then things began to fall apart.

Auntie Obama's mother, Auntie Yuki, died the year after Yaeko became a maiko, in 1939.

Auntie Oima took over as leader of the Iwasaki family. Yoneyu was still in active service and not ready to retire, so Auntie Oima had to put her aspirations of running a restaurant on hold and take over the Iwasaki okiya.

That was around the time my sister Kuniko entered the Iwasaki household. Kuniko was my parents' third-oldest daughter, and she was in elementary school at the time. She possessed a loving and nurturing demeanor, but two weaknesses kept her from becoming a maiko. The first was that she had poor vision and couldn't navigate the world without glasses. The second issue was that she had inherited my mother's figure, which was short and overweight. So, given her eyesight and amplitude, the authorities determined she should train as a support person rather than a geiko. She was sent to public school and began working as Aba's helper.

On December 8, 1941, Japan entered World War II, which lasted four years and caused terrible hardship in Gion Kobu and throughout the country. In order to concentrate the nation's resources and attention on the war effort, the government shuttered the Gion Kobu for commerce in 1943. Many geiko returned home to their families. Those who remained were assigned to labor in a munitions factory.

The Iwasaki okiya lacked indigo-dyed kimono (such as those worn by laborers), so they fashioned work uniforms from their old geiko robes. They must have appeared weird to those outside the karyukai. Work clothing was usually made of cotton, never the flimsy silk. Auntie Oima informed me years later that even though it was wartime, those of us who lived in Gion Kobu raced to see who had the most beautiful silk work garments. We had collars around our necks, two long braids in our hair, and crisp white headbands. We still wanted to feel feminine. We became famous for standing in line with our heads held high to work in the factory."

Auntie Oima split the okoya's belongings into three lots and delivered them to a different location for safety.

Auntie Oima only permitted the nucleus of the family, Yoneyu, Masako, Yaeko, and Kuniko, to remain in the okiya. She returned the surviving maiko and geiko to their parents. The city has run out of food. Auntie Oima and Kuniko informed me they were frightened they might go hungry. They lived on a limited diet of scavenged roots and a thin gruel made from water, salt, and a few grains.

Yaeko's partner, Seizo, became an officer and was stationed in Japan during the war, during which they maintained their relationship. In 1944, she stated that she was leaving to marry him. She hadn't yet paid back the money the Iwasaki okiya had put into her profession, but Auntie Oima didn't want to argue with her. She chose to accept the loss and kindly released Yaeko out of her contract. This type of breach is not uncommon, but it is in really terrible shape. She simply turned her back and walked away.

Yaeko was legally a member of the Iwasaki family, so Auntie Oima treated her as a daughter and gave her off with a decent dowry. It had jewelry, including the ruby presented to her by the Baron, as well as two enormous dressing chests containing fine kimono and obi. Yaeko relocated to Osaka and started a new life.

In December of the same year, the Iwasaki okiya received another hit. Yoneyu died abruptly from kidney disease. She was only 52. Auntie Oima was left without a replacement. Masako, at 22, was left without a mother.

Both Iwasaki okiya's stars had gone out.

The conflict concluded on August 15, 1945. The Iwasaki okiya had reached an all-time low. There were just three women residing in the large mansion. Auntie Oima is aging, Masako is despondent, and Kuniko is overweight. That was it. Auntie Oima told me she was at her wits end and was considering closing the okiya completely.

But then things started to look better. The American Occupation Forces ordered Gion Kobu to reopen, and the karyukai gradually returned to life. The Americans used a portion of the Kaburenjo Theater as a dance club. The military officers began to patronize the ochaya. A number of the geiko and maiko who had fled during the war asked if they may return to the okiya, including Koyuki, the Iwasaki geiko with the most supporters. Aba returned to work. The Iwasaki okiya was back in operation.

I questioned Auntie Oima if it was tough to welcome the Americans into the ochaya when we had just lost the war. She said that it wasn't as simple. Although there was considerable animosity, the cops were generally friendly. Most folks were content just to have the business. The karyukai's ability to serve all valued guests equally and without discrimination is firmly embedded in their psyches. But she did tell me a story that appeared to reflect her actual feelings.

Koyuki was summoned one night to attend General MacArthur's

banquet at the Ichiriki Tei. He was so taken with the kimono she was wearing that he requested if he might take it with him back to the United States.

The proprietor of Ichirikitei forwarded the request to Auntie Oima, who responded: "Our kimono are our lives. He is free to take the kimono, but he must accompany me. He may occupy my country, but never my soul!"

The proprietor of Ichiriki Tei relayed the response to the general, and he never requested the kimono again. When Auntie Oima told me this story, she raised her chin in the air and smiled. One of my favorite qualities about her was her sense of pride.

I still own the kimono. It is safely stored in a chest in my home.

The Iwasaki okiya, like the rest of Japan, battled forward for the following few years.

Masako was still waiting for her fiancé to return home from the war. The authorities did not notify Chojiro's family about his death until 1947. Masako was devastated. She grieved for days while hugging her marriage quilt to her chest. She was suddenly completely alone, with no future prospects and nowhere to go.

Masako made the decision to become a geiko after extensive conversations with Auntie Oima. She made her jikata (musician) geiko debut in 1949, at the age of twenty-six, under the name Fumichiyo.

Despite her beauty, Fumichiyo lacked the ability to enchant customers. She lacked the lighthearted artifice and sense of humor that a successful geiko requires. Being a geiko is more than just mastering your art form. One must also be passionate and enthusiastic about the career, which necessitates a deep dedication, a tremendous amount of labor, an unwavering demeanor, and the presence of mind to remain calm in the face of calamity.

None of this describes Masako. But, believing she had no other option, she persisted. And then she encountered additional hardship. Soon after starting employment, she contracted tuberculosis and had to halt for more than a year. She returned to work in the early 1950s, but her sporadic efforts did little to enhance the household's overall finances.

Kuniko had reached the marriageable age of eighteen. Inquiries were made, and plans were explored, but Kuniko refused to accept any proposals. In light of Yaeko's desertion, she felt compelled to remain in the Iwasaki okiya in order to protect my family's honor. Kuniko worked at the Iwasaki okiya for the next thirty years. She was single her entire life.

At this stage, the Iwasaki okiya could hardly support itself. The home had an impressive collection of costumes and an entire staff trained to dress geiko in them, but there weren't enough geiko to wear them. There weren't enough geiko to carry out the entire procedure. Auntie Oima needed to recruit new talent if the Iwasaki okiya was going to survive. That is what prompted her to come speak with my parents about Tomiko in the winter of 1952.

And, with Yoneyu and Yaeko gone, she needed to decide a successor.

CHAPTER 4
GROWING INTO GRACE

I started elementary school at the age of six, a year after beginning dancing training. Because the school was situated in Gion Kobu, many of the students were from families with direct involvement in the karyukai.

Kuniko was busy assisting Aba in the mornings, so one of our two maids, either Kaachan or Suzu-chan, drove me to school. (Chan is the universal diminutive in Japanese.) The school was located two short blocks north of Iwasaki okiya, off Hanamikoji.

This was the time of day I performed my "shopping." It was fairly simple. I went into the store and chose what I wanted or needed. The maid said, "It's for the Iwasakis of Shinbashi," and the shopkeeper handed me the item. A pencil. An eraser. A ribbon for my hair.

I had no idea what money was. For years, I assumed that all you had to do to receive something was ask for it. If you said, "It's for the Iwasakis of Shinbashi," you could obtain anything.

I was getting used to the fact that I was kind of an Iwasaki. But then, during my first year of school, Old Meanie showed up there on Parents' Day instead of my mother and father. She donned a light purple kimono with a sharkskin pattern and a sophisticated black haori (a jacket-like garment worn over the kimono). She wore thick makeup and a strong perfume. Every time she flapped her fan, a mist of smell filled the room. It was quite upsetting.

The next day, my classmates referred to me as "Little Miss geiko" and informed me that I was adopted. I became enraged since that wasn't true.

Kuniko took Old Meanie's place at the next parents' gathering at school because she was too busy. That made me a lot happier.

I enjoyed going to school. I enjoyed learning things. But I was horribly bashful and stayed to myself. The professors made an extra effort to engage me in play. Even the principal attempted to draw me out of my shell.

There was one little kid I liked. Her name was Hikari, or Sunbeam. She had an unusual appearance. Her hair was golden blond. I thought she was quite pretty.

Hikari did not have any pals either. I approached her, and we began playing together. We spent hours whispering and laughing under the ginkgo tree on the playground. I would have given anything to have hair like hers.

Most days, I rushed out of school as soon as the bell rang, eager to get to my dance class. I had the maid clean up my desk and ran home ahead of her. But once in a while, the dance teachers were preoccupied with something else, and we had the afternoon off.

When I wasn't busy, Hikari-chan invited me to come over after school. I intended to go straight home but opted to accompany her instead.

Kaachan arrived to take me up that day. She was a gossip and a thief. Darn it, I thought. I suppose I'll just have to trust her. "Kaachan, there's something I need to do. Please go take a cup of tea, and I will see you in an hour. And promise me you will not inform Auntie Oima. Understand?"

Hikari-chan lived alone with her mother in a small row house surrounded by neighbors. "How terribly convenient," I recall thinking, "to have everything and everyone so close by." Hikari's mother was kind and welcoming. She gave us an afterschool snack. I didn't normally eat snacks. My elder brothers and sisters were constantly scrambling for whatever was available, so I never ate anything. In this situation, I made an exception.

The time passed by, and I soon had to depart.

I returned to Kaachan, and she took me home. As soon as we arrived, it was clear that word of my whereabouts had already spread.

Auntie Oima chastised me badly. "I forbid you to go there again," she cried. Do you understand, young lady? Never ever again!"

I wasn't used to talking back to mom, but her fury perplexed me, so I tried to explain. I told her about Hikari-chan, how sweet her mother was, how they lived with all these nice people, and how much fun I had while I was there. But she refused to hear what I had to say. It was my first interaction with prejudice, and I honestly didn't get it.

There is a group of people in Japan known as burakumin. They are regarded as dirty and lowly, similar to the untouchables of India. Historically, this group cared for the deceased and dealt with various "polluted" things such as cattle and leather. They were undertakers, butchers, and shoemakers. The burakumin are no longer as isolated as they once were, but they were still mostly restricted to ghettos while I was growing up.

I had unknowingly crossed a line. Not only was Hikari-chan an outcast, but she was also a half-breed, fathered out of wedlock by an American GI. Auntie Oima was terrified that I might be polluted by association. One of her primary concerns was maintaining my good reputation. As a result of my harmless "transgression," there was widespread frenzy.

I was quite frustrated and vented my rage on poor Kaachan for tattling. I am afraid I made her life unpleasant for a spell. But I began to feel sad for her. She hailed from an impoverished family with many brothers and sisters. I caught her stealing tiny stuff from the house to send them. Instead of telling her, I offered her small gifts so she wouldn't have to steal.

Hikari-chan and her mother moved away shortly after the incident. I frequently wondered what happened to her.

But my life was too full to dwell on anything for long. When I was seven, I realized I was a "very busy person." I was always on the go, doing something, or seeing someone. I felt compelled to complete whatever I was doing as soon as possible and taught myself to be incisive and efficient. I was in a constant haste.

My longest sprint of the day happened between the end of school and the start of dance class. I got out of school at 2:30. Dance lessons began at 3:00, and I wanted to be early, preferably by 2:45. So I rushed back to the okiya. Kuniko had my dance clothing ready and changed me from Western to kimono. Then I bolted out the door. Kuniko, holding my dancing bag, followed behind me.

By this point, I had become quite connected to Kuniko and was as protective of her as she was of me. I despised it when others treated her as if she was lesser. Yaeko was the worst offender. She called Kuniko derogatory names like "pumpkin face" and "mountain monkey," which enraged me, but I had no idea how to deal with it.

Kuniko was responsible for transporting me to and from dancing class. She never skipped a day, no matter how busy she was at the okiya. I developed a series of regular rituals that I followed on my journey to and from dancing school. Kuniko patiently suffered from my routine. I had three things to complete on the way to class.

First, I had to deliver a piece of molasses candy to Mother Sakaguchi's home. (I came up with this concept on my own and implemented it.) In exchange, Mother Sakaguchi provided me with food. I saved the snack in my bag for later.

Next, I had to visit the shrine and pray.

Third, I had to rush and pet Dragon, the large white dog who lived in the florist business.

Then I could attend class.

Kuniko was constantly waiting to take me back to the okiya. I really enjoyed the ride home.

First, we went to the floral business, where I fed Dragon the food Mother Sakaguchi had given me. Then I looked around the store. I enjoyed the flowers because they reminded me of my mother. The girl in the shop let me choose one in exchange for bringing Dragon a treat. I thanked her and delivered the bouquet to the owner of the take-out gourmet shop down the street. In return, she sliced two slices of dashimaki, a delicious omelet shaped like a jelly roll, and gave them to me to go home.

Dashimaki was Auntie Obama's favorite snack. When I proudly presented her the package, she always smiled with excitement and pretended surprise. Every day. Then she broke into song. When she was happy, she would sing a famous jingle called su-isu-isu-daradattasurasurasuisuisui. To mislead me, she would insert an erroneous consonant, which I had to rectify before she ate the dashimaki. Then I'd sit down and tell her what I'd done that day.

My life began to revolve around going to Shinmonzen, and I sought to spend as much time as possible at the school. With each passing day, I grew more passionate about dancing and resolved to become a truly excellent dancer.

One day, I came to Shinmonzen and overheard Big Mistress conversing with someone in her studio. I was disappointed because I preferred to take the first lesson. When I entered the room, I noticed that the woman, albeit older, was lovely. There was something about how she handled herself. I was instantly intrigued.

Big Mistress told me to participate in the lesson. The older woman bowed and greeted me. Big Mistress taught us a dance called Ebony Hair. We practiced it several times. The woman was an excellent dancer. I was first self-conscious when dancing with her, but I quickly lost myself in the flow of the moves.

Big Mistress critiqued my job as usual. "That is very slow, Mine-chan. Increase the speed." "Your arms are sloppy." Make them tighter." She didn't say anything to the other woman.

After we finished, Big Mistress presented me to the guest. Her name was Han Takehara.

Madame Takehara was regarded as one of the greatest dancers of her period. She was a master in a variety of schools who cut to the heart of the medium by pioneering her own unique style. I was honored to have danced alongside her.

From a young age, I enjoyed observing accomplished dancers and searched out opportunities to train with them. This is one of the reasons I spent so much time at Shinmonzen: dancers traveled from all across Japan to study with the iemoto. Some of the women I met in those early years are now the iemoto of their respective schools. Of course, I spent numerous hours monitoring Inoue professors and students during their lessons.

A few months after my first (flawed) presentation, I was chosen to perform as a youngster in the Onshukai Dances, which took place in the fall. This was my first appearance on a public stage. The following spring, I performed in the Miyako Odori and continued to dance children's roles until I was eleven. Being on stage was an excellent learning opportunity since I was able to feel and experience the dancers up close.

Auntie Oima, unbeknownst to me, invited my parents to each of my performances, and as far as I know, they always showed there. My vision was so terrible that I couldn't make out anyone in the audience, but I knew they were there. My heart called out to them, "Look at me, Mom and Dad! Look at me dancing! Aren't I getting better?"

In Japan, Saturdays are school days, therefore Sunday was my only day off.

Instead of sleeping in, I got up early and hurried over to Shinmonzen since it was so much fun to see what the iemoto and tiny mistresses were up to in the morning. Some days I arrived at six a.m. (After I returned from the studio, I said my prayers and cleaned the toilets.) Children's courses began at eight o'clock on Sunday, so I had plenty of time to follow the tiny mistresses and see what they were doing.

Big Mistress began by praying, like Auntie Oima had done. While she was in the altar chamber, the tiny mistresses cleaned the school. They washed down the wood surfaces of the stage and the long passageways with rags and scrubbed the restrooms. I was impressed. Even though they were my teachers, they had to stick to the same regimen as me because they were still Big Mistress's disciples.

Big Mistress and the Little Mistresses ate breakfast together. Then Big Mistress taught the small mistresses, and I got to watch. This was the highlight of my week.

I also appreciated Kyoto's hot and humid summers. Every warm day, as part of my training, I had to sit behind Big Mistress and use a large circular paper fan to cool her. I enjoyed my job. It was an excellent opportunity to watch her teach for extended periods of time. The other girls didn't enjoy it as much, but I could sit there for hours. Big Mistress eventually forced me to take a rest. The other females played paper, scissors, and rock to determine who would take the following turn. Ten minutes later, I was back to fanning.

Along with the dance, I was focusing on my music. When I was ten years old, I put the koto away and started learning the shamisen, a stringed instrument with a square body and a long neck that is played with a plectrum. Shamisen music is the traditional accompaniment of Kyoto-style dance, especially the Inoue School. Studying the music enabled me to understand the movement's delicate patterns.

In Japanese, the word for dance is written as two words. One is Mai, and the other is Odori.

Mai is a sanctified movement originated from sacred dances done by Shrine maidens as tributes to the gods since ancient times. It can only be performed by persons who have been taught and permitted to do so. Odori, on the other hand, is a dance that celebrates the ups and downs of human life, commemorating happy milestones while solemnizing sorrowful ones. It is a popular dance during Japanese festivals and can be performed by anyone.

Mai refers to just three types of dance: mikomai (dances of Shinto shrine maidens), bugaku (dances of the imperial court), and noh mai (dances of Noh drama). Mai, not odori, refers to Kyoto-style dance. The Inoue School is specifically related with noh mai and shares stylistic characteristics.

By the age of ten, I had become aware of these discrepancies. I felt proud to be a mai dancer and Inoue School member. I was perhaps a touch too proud. I became a stickler for details.

One frigid winter day, I arrived at the studio and went to the hibachi to warm up. There was a teenage girl in the room that I had never seen before. Her haircut and what she was wearing indicated that she was a shikomisan.

Shikomisan refers to someone who is in the first stage of their apprenticeship to become a geiko, specifically one who is contracted to an okiya. For example, I was never referred to as a shikomisan since I am an atotori.

The shikomisan was sitting in the coldest portion of the room, next to the door. "Come sit next to the fire," I told her. "What is your name?""

"Tazuko Mekuta."

"I'll call you Meku-chan."

I believed she was around five or six years older than myself. However, at the Inoue School, seniority is established by the date of matriculation, not biological age. So, she was my "junior."

I took off my tab. "Meku-chan, my little toe itches."

I extended my foot, and she rubbed it with affection.

Meku-chan was nice and compassionate, with the most beautiful eyes. She reminded me of my older sister, Yukiko. I immediately fell in love.

Unfortunately, she only attended the school for a short time. I missed her and hoped to meet a companion like her. So I was thrilled later that winter when I returned to the hibachi and noticed a new girl about Meku-chan's age seated there. But when I entered the room, this girl was already curled up to the brazier, and she ignored me. She did not even say hello. This was inexcusable given her status as a novice.

"You can't sit next to the hibachi," I finally stated.

"So why not?" She responded indifferently."

"What is your name, anyway?" I asked.

"My name is Toshimi Suganuma." She did not say, "How are you doing?"

I was annoyed, but I also felt it was my obligation as her "senior" to give her the gift of my superior knowledge and explain how things worked at the Inoue School.

I attempted to make a point.

"When did you begin taking lessons?"

I wanted her to understand that I had been there longer than she had, and that she was expected to treat me with respect.

But she did not understand. "Oh, I don't know. I suppose it was a while ago.

When she was taken away for her lesson, I was trying to think of anything to say to help her recognize her shortcomings.

This was a serious issue. I'd have to discuss it with Auntie Oima.

I left school as soon as my lesson ended and finished my dog, flower, dashimaki ritual as swiftly as possible. I ran the remainder of the way home.

I handed the dashimaki to Auntie Oima. She appeared to be going to sing, but I stopped her. "Do not do suisui today. I have a problem and need to speak with you." I detailed my situation.

"Mineko, Toshimi will make her debut before you, so she will eventually become one of your big sisters. This requires you to respect her. And be polite to her. There's no reason for you to tell her what to do. I am confident that Big Mistress will teach Toshimi everything she needs to know. "It is not your responsibility."

I forgot about this occurrence till many years later. Soon after my debut as a maiko, I was invited to entertain at a dinner. Yuriko

(Meku-chan) and Toshimi, both of whom had become top-tier geiko, were in attendance. They made lighthearted jokes about how self-centered I had been as a child. I blushed blazing scarlet with embarrassment. However, they did not hold it against me. Both became major mentors to me in subsequent years. Yuriko became one of my only buddies.

Relationships in Gion Kobu are long-lasting, and harmony is valued more than any other societal ideal. Though the emphasis on peaceful cooperation is common across Japanese society, it is especially strong in the karyukai. I feel there are two explanations for this. The first is that our lives are so closely linked. People have no option but to get along.

The other explanation is in the nature of the business. Maiko and geiko entertain influential people from all walks of life and from throughout the world. We are de facto diplomats and must be able to interact with everyone. But this does not imply that we are doormats. We are supposed to have keen wit and insight. Over time, I learnt how to convey my thoughts and opinions without offending people.

CHAPTER 5
A SILENT GOODBYE

When I turned ten in November 1959, I had to appear before Family Court again. Old Meanie snatched me. My parents were present when I arrived. I had a lawyer named Mr. Kikkawa. He had oily hair yet was the best lawyer in Kyoto.

I was supposed to tell the judge where I wanted to live.

The anxiety of having to make a decision was terrible. When I thought of my parents, my heart ached. My father leaned over to me, saying, "You don't have to do it, Masako. You are not obligated to stay with them if you do not wish to. I nodded. Then it happened again. I vomited right there in the courtroom.

This time, the judge did not halt the proceedings.

Instead, he looked me in the eye and asked directly.

"Which family do you want to belong to, the Tanakas or the Iwasakis?"

I stepped up, took a big breath, and stated clearly, "I'm going to belong to the Iwasakis."

"Are you absolutely sure that is what you want?"

"Yes, I am."

I had previously decided what I was going to say, but I felt terrible as the words came out of my mouth. I felt bad for hurting my parents. But I said what I said because I enjoy dancing. That is what swayed the scales in the Iwasakis' favor. The dance had become my life, and I couldn't imagine abandoning it for anything or anyone. I opted to become an Iwasaki so that I could keep studying to dance.

I walked out of the courthouse with my parents, holding each other's hands. I couldn't bear to look at any of them since I felt so guilty about my treachery. I cried. Out of the corner of my eye, I noticed my parents crying.

Old Meanie hails a cab, and the four of us return to the okiya.

My father attempted to soothe me. "Maybe this is all for the best, Ma-chan," remarked the man. "I'm sure you have more pleasure living at the Iwasaki okiya than you would at home. There are so many intriguing things to do there. But if you ever want to come home, just let me know and I'll come get you. Anytime. Day or night. "Just call me."

I glanced at him and said, "I've died."

My parents turned and walked away. They were both wearing kimonos. As their obis faded into the distance, I yelled out, "Dad! Mom!" in my heart. But the words never left my lips.

My father turned back to look at me. I resisted the need to run after him and, through tears, waved goodbye. I'd made my choice.

That night, Auntie Oima was overjoyed. It was official. I was now Iwasaki's successor. When the paperwork was completed, I would become the designated heir. We ate a large meal that included celebratory delicacies like sea bream and red bean rice as well as more pricey cuisine like steak. Many individuals came to express their congratulations and bring me gifts.

The party lasted for hours. I couldn't take it any longer and walked to the closet. Auntie Oima couldn't stop chanting "Susu-isu-dararat asurasurasu suisui." Even Old Meanie was laughing aloud. Everyone was happy, including Aba, Mother Sakaguchi, and the okasan of the branch households. Even Kuniko.

I'd just said goodbye to my mother and father. For good. I could not comprehend that everyone saw this as a reason to celebrate. I was fatigued, and my mind was completely blank. Without thinking, I took one of my hair's black velvet ribbons, wrapped it around my neck, pulled as hard as I could, and attempted suicide. It did not work. Finally, discouraged, I gave up and collapsed into a pool of tears.

The next morning, I concealed the bruise on my neck and dragged myself to school. I felt absolutely empty. I somehow made it through the morning and forced myself to attend dancing class.

When I arrived, Big Mistress asked me what dance we were working on. "Yozakura ['cherry blossoms at night']," I answered.

"All right then, show me what you remember."

I started to dance.

She began angrily reprimanding me. "That's not right, Mineko. And that. And that! Stop it Mineko, what's wrong with you today? Stop it! Stop right now; do you hear me? Don't you dare cry. I hate it when small girls weep. "You are dismissed!"

I could not believe it. I didn't know what I had done wrong. I wasn't crying, but I was quite perplexed. I started apologizing, but she wouldn't answer, so I left.

I'd just gotten my first, dreaded OTOME, and I had no idea why.

Otome, which translates as "Stop!" is a penalty particular to the Inoue School. When the teacher gives you an otome, you must instantly stop and exit the studio. And she doesn't say when you'll be permitted to return, so it's an endless suspension. The thought of being prevented from continuing to dance was excruciatingly painful.

I didn't wait for Kuniko; instead, I walked home alone and went right into the closet, saying nothing to anyone. I was miserable. First the courtroom, and now this. Why was Big Mistress so angry?

Auntie Oima approached the closet door.

"What happened to Mine-chan?" "Why did you come home alone?"

"Mine-chan, will you be having dinner?"

"Mine-chan, would you like to take a bath?"

I declined to respond.

I heard one of the Sakaguchi maids enter the room. She explained that Mother Sakaguchi needs to see Auntie Oima straight away. Auntie Oima raced away.

Mother Sakaguchi got directly to the point. "We are in a bit of a problem. Ms. Aiko has just called. Apparently, her assistant mixed up the titles of two works, one that Mineko had just completed and one that she was learning. Miss Kawabata explained to Mineko that Sakuramiyotote ["cherry blossom viewing"] meant Yozakura ["cherry blossoms at night"], and vice versa. So Mineko did the wrong dance today, and Aiko gave her an otome. Is Mineko alright?"

"So that is what occurred. No, she's not fine. She's in the closet and won't speak to me. I suppose she's quite upset."

"What are we going to do if she threatens to quit?"

"We'll have to convince her not to."

"Go home and do your best to get her out of the closet."

I assumed that I must have gotten the otome because I wasn't trying hard enough, and that I simply needed to improve. So, right there in the closet, I began to rehearse both the dance I was learning and the dance I had just finished. I practiced them for hours. I kept reminding myself to concentrate. If I perform things flawlessly tomorrow, Big Mistress will be so surprised that she may forget about the otome.

However, as with many things in Gion Kobu, it was not that easy. I couldn't simply return to class as if nothing had happened. It didn't really matter who was at fault. I had received the otome, and my elders had to petition for my continuing enrollment. We set off for Shinmonzen. Mother Sakaguchi, Aunt Oima, Mistress Kasama, Old Meanie, Yaeko, Kun-chan, and myself.

Mother Sakaguchi bows and addresses Big Mistress. "I sincerely apologize for the regrettable event that occurred yesterday. We implore you to allow Mineko to continue attending your prestigious institution."

Nobody mentioned anything about what had truly transpired. The reason didn't matter. What was vital was that everyone save face and that I be able to continue my training uninterrupted.

"Very good, Mother Sakaguchi, I'll do as you ask. Mineko, please show us what you're working on.

I danced to Cherry Blossom Viewing. Then, without being asked, I performed Cherry Blossoms At Night. I performed well. When I finished, the room became quiet. I gazed around, noting the range of emotions on the women's faces.

It struck me that the adult world was extremely difficult.

I now see that Big Mistress used the otome as an effective teaching tool. She gave me an otome anytime she wanted to force me to advance to the next level of artistry; she purposefully exploited the dread of the otome to energize my spirit. It was a test. Will I be back stronger? Or will I give up and quit? I don't think this is a terribly intelligent educational concept, but it has always worked for me.

Big Mistress never handed otome to mediocre dancers; instead, she groomed us for significant parts. The only person who faced any real consequences from my first otome was the teacher who had given me incorrect information. She was never permitted to tutor me again.

My adoption was formally finalized on April 15, 1960. I had been living in the Iwasaki okiya for the past five years, so the change in status had no impact on my everyday routine. Except that now I had to sleep upstairs in Old Meanie's chamber.

I'd come all the way across the bridge. My childhood home was behind me. The world of dance lay ahead.

CHAPTER 6
SNOW

Auntie Oima, who was ninety-two years old, fell ill unexpectedly in November 1964 and was confined to her futon. My sixteenth birthday has come and gone. I stayed by her side as much as possible, talking to her and rubbing her aged and worn muscles. She refused to let anyone but Kuniko or me bathe her or change her bedpan.

Gion Kobu begins its New Year preparations in mid-December, before the rest of the country does. We begin on December 13, which we call Kotohajime.

The first order of business on Kotohajime is to pay a visit to the iemoto for a traditional exchange of greetings and presents. The iemoto gives everyone of us a new fan for the upcoming year. The hue of the fan corresponds to our current ranking. In exchange, we give her two items in the name of our family: okami san, a pair of pounded glutinous rice cakes stacked on top of each other, and a red and white envelope holding money. The envelope is decorated with beautiful gold and silver twine. The quantity of money is related to the "price" of the fan we received, or our position in the school hierarchy: less for children, more for senior geiko. When Kotohajime is finished, the iemoto gives the sweets and money to a school for physically disabled or mentally retarded children.

On December 13, I dressed and proceeded to make my Kotohajime visit. I recall feeling a little nostalgic. This was my final year as an amateur. I was supposed to take the maiko examination the next autumn when I was sixteen, and if I passed, I'd start my professional career.

So I was taken aback when Big Mistress nodded at me and added,

"Mine-chan, there is an exam at the Nyokoba the day after tomorrow that I want you to take. It starts at ten o'clock, so please arrive by nine thirty."

I had no choice but to comply, even though I didn't want to cope with another issue on top of Auntie Oima's illness. I returned home and informed Auntie Oima the news. I couldn't believe how she changed. She felt like her old self again. Her face erupted into a grin, and she began singing the suisui tune. For the first time, I realized how vital it was for Auntie Oima that I become a maiko. It was a powerful epiphany. I had really not been paying attention.

Old Meanie arrived home in the middle of a banquet. Auntie Oima briefed her about the exam. Old Meanie was even more excited than Auntie Oima.

"Oh, goodness. That leaves us with very little time. Kuniko, please cancel my engagements for the rest of the day. Consider canceling tomorrow and the next day as well. Okay, Mineko, let us get to work. First, phone two of the girls and invite them to come over. It's best to practice in groups. Go, hurry, we need to get started."

I tried not to giggle at her pompousness.

"But I won't take the exam for real until next year. This one is not a huge deal. "I basically know the dances."

"Stop talking crap. We need to get to work, and we don't have much time. Now, call your friends. "And be quick about it."

I still didn't see the point, but I performed as instructed.

The girls were grateful for the extra attention.

We were asked to prepare seven pieces. Old Meanie brought out her shamisen and started playing. We practiced every item hundreds of times. We worked all day and night, scarcely stopping for food or sleep. By the end of the two days, I knew every tiny movement in all seven dances by heart. Old Meanie didn't stop for a minute. She was great.

On December 15, Old Meanie woke me up early to ensure that we were at the Nyokoba on time. Thirteen girls sat and waited in Studio 2. Everyone was quite nervous. Except for me. I still didn't understand the significance of the moment.

For some, today was their last chance. If they didn't pass the time, they'd have to abandon their goals of becoming maiko.

We were called in one by one for testing. We couldn't see what was happening behind the closed door. This simply contributed to the sense of unease in the corridor.

We wouldn't know which item we had to perform until we got inside and stood alone on the stage. Then the Big Mistress would tell us what to do.

Two of my friends came before me.

"What did you get?""I inquired about their release date.

"Torioi [the story of a strolling shamisen player]," they both said.

"Piece of cake," I thought. "I've got that one." I started dancing Torioi in my brain, methodically going over each and every motion. I didn't understand what everyone was so concerned about.

Then it was my turn.

The first element of the exam was opening the door. I did everything just as I was taught. By this point, mechanical movements had become second nature. They felt fluid and graceful.

I slid the door open, bowed, and requested permission to enter. I could understand why the other girls were so nervous. Big Mistress was not alone there. All the tiny mistresses were present. And the master of Ichiriki Tei. Members of the Kabukai. Also present were delegates from the Ochaya and Geiko associations. There were also other people I did not recognize. There were rows of people seated in front of the stage. Ready to pass judgment.

I tried to keep my cool and mounted the stage as calmly as I could.

The Big Mistress looked at me and said one word: "Nanoha [the story of a butterfly and a cole blossom]."

Oops, I thought. Not Torioi. Okay, this is it. Give it your best effort.

I hesitated for a second, said "thank you," greeted the judges, and then started dancing. I executed the first section of the piece flawlessly. But, just before the end, I made a minor error. I paused in the middle of my posture.

I turned to the accompanist and told him, "I made a mistake. Please start again from the top."

Big Mistress interrupted. "We would not have noticed if you hadn't said something. Excuse me, everyone, but since Mineko had almost finished the piece, would you mind if she just did the last section again?"

"Of course," they all replied.

"Mine-chan, just the last part please."

"Yes," I replied, and went on to finish the work.

I thanked the panel again and exited the stage.

Old Meanie paced the hallway like a cat. She pounced as soon as she spotted me. "How did it go?"

"I made a mistake."

"Is there a mistake?" What kind of error? Was it bad? Do you believe you failed?"

"For sure."

"Oh, dear, I hope not."

"Why?" I was still not taking the situation seriously.

"Because Auntie Oima would be devastated. She is lying there with bated breath, waiting for the findings. I hoped to give her good news."

Now I was feeling dreadful. I'd entirely forgotten about Auntie Oima. I wasn't just a bad dancer; I was also selfish and dishonest. The longer we waited, the worse I felt. Finally, a Kabukai member summoned us all to the entranceway of the Nyokoba.

"These are the results of today's exam. I am glad to announce that Miss Mineko Iwasaki won first place with a score of 97 points. Congratulations, Mineko.

He then proceeded to post a list on the wall. "Here are the remaining results. My apologies to all of you who did not make it.

I could not believe it. I assumed there had to be some sort of error. But there it was, in black and white.

"This couldn't be better," Old Meanie exclaimed with glee. "Auntie Oima will be ecstatic! Mineko, I am really proud of you. What an excellent achievement! Let's celebrate before we head home, shall we? Please ask your friends to join us. Where should we go? Anything you desire is fine. "It's on me." She was nearly babbling.

We took the gang to Takarabune for steak. It took forever to get there. Old Meanie must have bowed to everyone we passed along the road and said, "Mineko came in first!" Thank you very much!"

She was thanking everyone because she, like many Japanese, felt that it takes a village to raise a child. I was the result of a group effort rather than a single individual. And the group was called Gion Kobu.

The restaurant owners were old friends, and they overwhelmed us with food and congratulations. Everyone else was having a nice time, but I was unhappy. One of the girls asked me what was wrong.

"Just shut up and eat your steak," I told you.

I wasn't in a horrible mood. There were so many ideas and feelings flowing through my mind. I was relieved I passed the exam, but I felt horrible for those who failed. I was quite concerned about Auntie Oima. And I was thinking about my relationship with Old Meanie.

I'd been living in the Iwasaki okiya for ten years. Masako had welcomed me into the family nearly five years prior. I was thinking about how I'd never allowed myself to call her "Mother."

After the adoption papers arrived, I was playing with a water pistol and sprayed her in an attempt to gain attention. She rushed after me and shouted, "If you were my real child, I'd spank you." It was like a slap in the face. I assumed I was her child. In some ways, yeah. I didn't truly belong to my mother anymore. Who did I belong to?

When Masako was younger, Auntie Oima urged her to try to have a child. The karyukai promotes women's freedom, and there is no stigma associated with being a single mother. As I previously stated, it is easier to raise girls than boys in the karyukai, but many women have nurtured males as well. Auntie Oima, of course, hoped Masako would bear a girl, someone to carry on the family name, an atotori.

However, Masako refused to consider it. She had never really accepted the fact that she was illegitimate and did not want to put anyone else in the same situation. She was also physically weakened as a result of tuberculosis. She wasn't convinced she had the strength to bear a child.

When I was adopted, I vowed that I would never call Old Meanie "Mother." But now I'm not so sure. How about the past two days? How hard had she worked for me? How much did she want me to succeed? A true mother couldn't have done more.

I considered changing my mind.

When we finished our lunch, I took the plunge. I looked at her directly and said, "Mom, let's go home."

The look of surprise on her face was fleeting, but it will stay with me. "Yes, shall we?""She grinned. "Thank you for coming. I'm very glad you could join us.

We walked back to Iwasaki Okiya. "This has been one of the best days of my life," she told me.

We went inside Auntie Oima's room to deliver the good news. I had the presence of mind to express my gratitude for all of her efforts on my behalf.

Auntie Oima was overjoyed, but attempted to remain calm: "I never doubted that you would pass. None at all. Now we need to plan your clothes. We will start tomorrow. Masako, we need to contact Eriman, Saito, and a number of others. Let's create a list. We have so much to accomplish!"

Auntie Oima died without missing a beat. This was her life's goal. And she promised that my debut would be amazing. I was glad she was happy, but I had conflicting feelings about being a maiko. I still wasn't sure it was what I wanted to do. It's true that I wanted to continue dancing. But I also wanted to attend high school.

Following the test, everything moved so swiftly that I had little time for self-reflection. It was already December 15. Mother Sakaguchi,

Auntie Oima, and Mama Masako agreed that I would become a minarai, or apprentice maiko, on February 15 and make my formal debut, or misedashi, on March 26.

Because I was becoming a maiko a year early, I would begin attending classes at the Nyokoba before graduating from junior high on March 15. And if I were to perform in next spring's Miyako Odori, I'd need to be available for press appearances beginning the following month.

The Iwasaki okiya was bustling with preparations for my debut as well as the arrival of the New Year. Our resources were stretched. Auntie Oima was bedridden and had to be looked after. The okiya needed to be carefully cleaned, from top to bottom. A steady stream of purveyors came in to consult on various areas of my outfit. Kun-chan, Aba, and Mama Masako were all busy, so I spent every free moment with Auntie Oima instead. Tomiko stopped by frequently to join in the mayhem. She was pregnant with the first of her two sons, but she graciously assisted in making arrangements for my coming out.

I was aware that the time I spent with Auntie Oima was valuable. She made a point of expressing to me how glad she was that I had opted to address Masako as mother. "Mineko, I understand Masako is a difficult person, but she is a really excellent one. She has such a pure heart that she can come across as overly serious and forthright. However, you can always trust her. So please be nice to her. She has no wicked bones in her body. "Not like Yaeko."

I tried my best to reassure her. I understand, Auntie Oima. Please do not worry about us. We will be alright. Let me give you a massage."

A minarai is only for a month or two. Minarai refers to learning via observation. This is a chance for the aspiring maiko to obtain direct experience with the ochaya. She wears professional attire and attends nightly banquets. She watches the subtle nuances of behavior, etiquette, demeanor, and conversational skills that she will soon have to exhibit.

The minarai is sponsored by an ochaya (her minaraijaya), although she is welcome to attend feasts at other locations. Every evening, she gets dressed and reports to her ochaya for work. The owner schedules her engagements. This is convenient because the owner, as mentor, is on-site to address any questions that may occur. It is not uncommon for the owner and minarai to form a long-term bond.

When I passed the unexpected exam, my elders had to decide which ochaya would care for me. They had several possibilities. Sakaguchi women were traditionally apprenticed at the Tomiyo, the Iwasakis at the Maniku, and Yaeko at the Minomatsu. For some reason, my elders selected the Fusanoya for me. I am convinced the reason was related to Gion Kobu politics at the time.

On January 9, the Kabukai distributed a confidential document containing the names of the geiko who will participate in that year's Miyako Odori. My name appeared among them. It was now official.

I was told that the picture shoot for the advertising brochure will take place on January 26. This meant that the Iwasaki okiya needed to put together a genuine ensemble for me to wear by that date. The already rapid pace of preparations became a frenzy.

On January 21, I returned from my dance class and proceeded to spend the day with Auntie Oima. As if she had been waiting for me to arrive home, she died as soon as I sat down next to her. Kun-chan was also there. We were both too shocked to cry. I refused to accept she was truly gone.

Auntie Oima's funeral was in black and white, as if it were an old movie. It was a brutally cold morning. Snow was falling. The ground was carpeted in white. Hundreds of mourners gathered at the Iwasaki okiya. They all wore solemn black mourning kimonos.

A cloth runner connected the genkan to the altar room. The entire surface was covered in a 3-inch-high salt carpet. It was a road of pure white salt.

Mama Masako sat in the front of the room. I sat next to her. Kuniko sat next to me. The casket sat in front of the altar. The Buddhist priests sat in front of the casket, reciting sutras.

Following the funeral, we followed the casket to the Crematory. We waited for two hours while they burned her. We then collected some of her burnt bones using special chopsticks and placed them in an urn. The ashes were white. We carried the urn back to the Iwasaki okiya and set it on the altar. The priests returned, and the family held a private service.

The day's sharp contrasts seemed to portray Auntie Obama's life with tremendous clarity and dignity.

Mama Masako was now the owner of the Iwasaki okiya.

We kept working on my coming out. I had to prepare to participate in the planned picture session on January 26, the seventh day after Auntie Oima's death and the day of her first memorial ceremony.

That morning, Mother Sakaguchi arrived at the okiya to do my makeup. I sat in front of her, feeling majestic and grown-up with my first formal hairstyle. She stared at me with an achingly sensitive look of pride. Auntie Oima was no longer alive. I burst into tears. I cried for two hours before Mother Sakaguchi could begin to apply my makeup, keeping everyone waiting.

Auntie Oima's urn was interred 49 days after her death at the Iwasaki burial in Otani Cemetery.

CHAPTER 7
A SYMPHONY OF TRADITIONS

The aesthetics of the Ochaya stem from the traditional Japanese tea ceremony, a hard artistic discipline better defined as "the way of tea."

Tea ceremonies are highly choreographed rituals that honor the simple act of sharing a cup of tea with a small group of friends, providing a welcome respite from the stresses of regular life. It takes a great deal of artifice to achieve the ideal simplicity of the tea ritual. The teahouse itself, as well as every handcrafted piece in it, are works of art that were meticulously created. The host prepares bowls of tea for his guests in a sequence of meticulously orchestrated and constantly practiced actions. There is nothing left to chance.

Similarly at the ochaya. Everything possible is done to guarantee that the guests enjoy an unforgettable experience. No details are ignored. An event at an ochaya is known as an ozashiki. This loosely translates as "banquet," or "dinner party," and is also the name of the private room where the event will be conducted.

An ozashiki is an opportunity for a host and his or her guests to enjoy the finest cuisine, relaxation, interesting discussion, and exquisite entertainment that the ochaya can offer. An ozashiki lasts a few hours, takes place in a completely private and beautiful setting, and, like the tea ceremony, should provide a respite from daily life. The ochaya provides the environment, the maiko and geiko serve as catalysts, but the guests' sophistication sets the tone for the evening.

An individual can only become a customer of an ochaya by personal referral. One cannot walk in from the street. Clients with a strong karyukai reputation introduce new customers to the system. This results in an intrinsic process of self-selection, in which any guest with the means to organize a feast in an ochaya in Gion Kobu is, practically by definition, trustworthy, learned, and sophisticated. Parents frequently accompany their young adult children to banquets as part of their schooling. A family may have a long-standing association with a particular ochaya.

A regular at the Gion Kobu develops a solid relationship with one ochaya. In some situations, a customer may visit two places, one for business entertainment and the other for informal socializing, although most customers use the same ochaya for both.

A strong sense of loyalty forms between an ochaya and its regular customers, many of whom host ozashiki at least once a week, if not more frequently. Similarly, clients form meaningful ties with their favorite geiko. We get to know our frequent customers well. Some of my most meaningful interactions began in the ozashiki. My best customers were professionals with extensive knowledge in a specific subject. The most pleasurable ozashiki for me were ones that taught me anything.

I liked some clients so much that I always made time to attend their ozashiki, no matter how busy my calendar was. Others I did my hardest to avoid. The bottom conclusion, however, is that the geiko has been employed to entertain the ozashiki host and his or her guests. She is there to make others feel wonderful. When a geiko enters an ozashiki, she must approach the person seated in the place of honor and engage them in conversation. No matter how she feels, her look must indicate, "I couldn't wait to come right over and speak to you." If her face says, "I can't stand you," she isn't cut out for the geiko role. It is her responsibility to discover something positive in everyone.

Sometimes I had to be kind to folks who I felt were physically disgusting. This was the most challenging because aversion is a difficult reaction to mask. However, the customers had paid for my company. The least I could do was treat each of them kindly. One of the most difficult aspects of the job is hiding one's real preferences and dislikes behind a façade of gentility.

Customers used to be art enthusiasts and students of shamisen, traditional art, or Japanese dance. They had so been schooled to grasp what they were witnessing and were eager to participate in the kind of dynamic artistic discussion that maiko and geiko excel at. Unfortunately, many wealthy people no longer have the time or motivation to continue such pastimes. The maiko and geiko, on the other hand, are beautiful and masterful in their own right, and anyone can appreciate them.

Conversation at a banquet is diverse, and geiko are expected to be educated about current events and contemporary literature, as well as well-versed in traditional art forms such as tea ceremony, flower arrangement, poetry, calligraphy, and painting. The first forty or fifty minutes of a banquet are often reserved for a pleasant discussion of these issues.

The banquet is served by serving women (naikai), who are aided by maids, with the geiko pouring sake. Needless to say, the cuisine must be exceptional. Ochaya do not prepare their own meals, instead relying on the area's many gourmet restaurants and catering services (shidashi) to offer feasts that are appropriate for the host's preferences and budget.

The cost of an ochaya banquet is high. An ozashiki costs approximately $500 per hour. This includes the usage of the room as well as the services provided by the Ochaya personnel. It excludes the requested meal and drink, as well as the geiko's service expenses. A two-hour party with a full dinner for a few people and three or four geikos can easily cost two thousand dollars.

The ochaya must meet the stringent requirements of consumers from the highest levels of Japanese and foreign society. The ochaya embodies the best of traditional Japanese architecture and interior design, having historically been built on the exquisite aesthetic of the tea ceremony. Each room must have a tatami floor and a tokonoma (alcove) decorated with the appropriate monthly hanging scroll and a floral arrangement in a fitting vase. These amenities are totally customized for each guest.

At some point, the geiko performs. There are primarily two types of geiko: tachikata and jikata. A tachikata is a major performer. She is trained to dance and play instruments other than the shamisen, such as the flute and hand drum. A jikata is a trained shamisen player and singer. Tachikata begin their training early and debut as maiko in their early teens, whereas jikata, who emerge as ordinary geiko, learn for a shorter amount of time and debut later (such as my sister Tomiko).

Physical beauty is required to become a tachikata, but not for jikata. Tachikata who do not develop into skilled dancers focus on becoming expert musicians.

The Iwasaki okiya was well-known for its drumming, and I began learning the tsutsumi hand drum as a child. Because of my renown as a dancer, I was rarely requested to play the tsutsumi at ozashiki, but I did it on stage every year during the Miyako Odori.

At a feast, a tachikata will dance. A jikata geiko will play the shamisen while singing. Following the performance, the conversation frequently turns to creative topics. The geiko may deliver a funny story or lead the party through a drinking game.

A geiko's cost is measured in units of time known as hanadai, or "flower charges," which are often calculated in fifteen-minute increments and billed to the client. In addition to hanadai, clients pay the geiko cash tips (goshugi), which they slip in small white envelopes and tuck into her obi or sleeve. She is allowed to retain them for herself.

At the end of the night, the ochaya computes the hanadai for all the maiko and geiko who attended the banquets that evening. They record the tallies on slips of paper and place them in a box in the ochaya's entrance. The next morning, a person from the kenban, or financial affairs office, goes around the ochaya collecting all of the slips from the previous night. These are tabulated and reported to the Kabukai. The kenban is an autonomous organization that provides this service on behalf of the Geiko Association.

The kenban checks with the okiya to ensure that the accounts are in agreement and, if no errors have occurred, calculates the revenue distribution. It informs the ochaya of the amount necessary to pay taxes and monthly fees. It then stipulates the sum that the ochaya must pay the okiya.

The ochaya, in turn, maintains its own accounts and invoices its consumers on a regular schedule. This was done once a year in the past, but it is currently done monthly. After receiving payment, the ochaya settles with the okiya.

The okasan of the okiya enters the sum received into the geiko's ledger, deducts fees and expenses, and transfers the balance to the geiko's account.

This open accounting system ensures that we know which geiko performed the most business on any given day. It is always evident who is number one.

February 15th was a huge day. I began rehearsals for the Miyako Odori, full-time lessons at the Nyokoba (I took the last month of junior high school off), and my apprenticeship as a minarai at the Fusanoya ochaya, which lasted approximately a month.

Mother Sakaguchi arrived at the okiya to supervise the dressing process and do my cosmetics herself.

It was quite the production.

A maiko in full costume closely resembles the Japanese concept of feminine beauty.

She has the traditional appearance of a Heian princess, as if she walked out of an 11th-century scroll painting. Her face is perfectly oval. Her complexion is white and faultless, and her hair is black as a raven's wing. Her eyebrows are half moons, and her mouth is a beautiful rosebud. Her neck is long and sensual, and her form is softly rounded.

I went to the hairdresser and had my hair done in the wareshinobu style, which is the first hairdo that a maiko wears. The hair is swept up and sculpted into a mass on the top of the head, fastened by red silk bands (kanoko) front and back and embellished with kanzashi, the stick pin ornaments that distinguish the karyukai style. This modest, beautiful style is considered to highlight the little girl's neck curve and the freshness of her features to their full potential.

After completing at the hairdresser, I proceeded to the barbershop to get my face shaved, which is a customary ritual for Japanese ladies. My father shaved my face for the first time, after giving me my first haircut, on the day I turned one. I've had it done once a month since then.

After becoming a maiko, I visited the hairdresser once every five days. To keep the contour of my haircut, I slept on a rectangle lacquered wooden pillow topped with a narrow cushion. The pillow initially kept me awake, but I quickly became accustomed to it. Other girls found things more challenging. The okiya had a method to keep us from removing the pillow at night. The servants would spread rice bran across the pillow. If a girl removed the pillow, particles of bran stuck like glue to the pomade in her hair, and she had to return to the hairdresser the next morning, upset.

I wore two hairpins tipped with silk plum blossoms (because it was February) on the sides of the bun's back, a pair of silver flutters (bira) on the sides in front, an orange blossom pin (tachibana) on top, and a long pin tipped with balls of red coral (akadama) and jade inserted horizontally through the base.

Mother Sakaguchi used the maiko's unique white cosmetics on my face and neck. This makeup has an intriguing history. Originally, male nobility wore it to audiences with the Emperor. In premodern times, the emperor was considered a hallowed presence and received his subjects behind a thin veil. The audience chamber was illuminated by candles. The white makeup reflected whatever light was there, making it simpler for the emperor to tell who was who.

Dancers and performers later adopted the practice. Not only does the white makeup look good on stage, but it also reflects the significance put on light skin. Previously, cosmetics contained zinc, which was extremely harmful to the skin. But that is no longer the case.

Mother Sakaguchi next applied pink powder on my cheeks and brows. She applied red lipstick to my bottom lip. (A year later, I started wearing lipstick on my top lip, too.) Then it was time to get ready.

A maiko wears a kimono known as a hikizuri. It differs from a standard kimono in that it has long sleeves, a big train, and is worn low on the back of the neck. The train's hem is weighted and curves out behind in a graceful arc. The hikizuri is fastened with a particularly long obi (about 20 feet long), which is tied in the back with both ends dangling down. A mineral's kimono is similar to that of a maiko, but the train and obi are not as long; the dangling portion of the obi is half the length of the maiko's.

My kimono was made of figured satin with variegated turquoise. The train's hefty hem was painted burnt orange, and against it floated a drift of pine needles, maple leaves, cherry blossoms, and chrysanthemum petals. My obi was made of black damask and adorned with swallowtail butterflies. I wore a silver obi clasp shaped like a swallowtail butterfly.

I carried a kago, a traditional handbag with a basketweave foundation topped with a drawstring purse of colorful tie dyed silk, shibori, which is created by tying silk into a myriad of minute knots with thread before dyeing. The end result is a beautiful dappled look. Kyoto is known for this method. My mother practiced it.

My handbag's shibori was pale peach, with a cabbage butterfly motif. It contained my dancing fan (decorated with the three red diamonds of the Konoe family [close advisers to the Emperor] painted on a gold background), a red-and-white hand towel with a matching design, a boxwood comb, and other accessories. All of these were encased in coverings made of the same silk as the bag and monogrammed.

Finally, I was dressed and ready to go. I stepped into my okobo as the maid slid open the front door. I was about to step over the lintel when I paused in surprise. The street was filled with people, shoulder to shoulder. There was no way I was going out in that.

I turned around in confusion.

"Kun-chan, I'm not sure what's going on, but there are a million people on the street." Can I wait until they are gone?"

"Do not be stupid, Mineko. They are coming to see you.

I knew people were looking forward to my debut as a maiko, but I had no clue about the degree. Many folks had waited years for this moment.

Voices called from outside:

Come out, Mineko! Let us see how stunning you are!"

"I cannot face all of those folks. "I'll just wait until the crowd thins."

"Mineko, these individuals aren't going anywhere. Ignore them if you must, but it's time to get going. "You cannot be late on your first day."

I still refused. I didn't want all those people staring at me. Kuniko was becoming frustrated. The walker from Fusanoya was waiting outside to accompany me. She was becoming annoyed. Kuniko was attempting to calm her while also getting me to move.

She finally read me the riot act. "You need to do it for Auntie Oima. This is what she'd always wanted. "Don't you dare disappoint her."

I knew she was correct. I had no choice.

I turned back toward the door. I took a long breath and thought, "Okay, Dad." Mom. Okay, Auntie Oima. Here I go! I let out a soft, resolute grunt before lifting my foot over the threshold.

Another bridge. Another passage.

The crowd erupted in loud applause. People called out congratulations and admiration, but I was too ashamed to hear them. I kept my face down and my eyes veiled the entire way to Fusanoya. The entire route was congested with well-wishers, and it was late by the time we made our way past them. I didn't see them, but I'm certain my parents were present.

The master (otosan, or father) of the ochaya quickly chastised me for being late. "There is no need for such tardiness, young lady, especially on your first day. It demonstrates a lack of dedication and focus. You are now a Minarai. "Act like one."

It was evident that he took his responsibility to me seriously.

"Yes, sir," I replied crisply.

"Stop using standard Japanese. Speak our language. Say 'hey' instead of 'hae.'"

"Hae, please forgive me."

"You mean 'hei, eraisunmahen.' Don't stop working on this until you sound like a proper geiko."

"Hae."

If you recall, this was the same critique I heard from Big Mistress when I was five. It took years for me to become really proficient in the district's mellifluous, artistically imprecise, and difficult-to-understand idioms. Now it's difficult for me to say anything else.

The okasan of the Fusanoya was more encouraging. "Do not worry, sweetheart. It may take some time, but I am confident you will learn it quickly. Simply do your best.

I responded positively to her friendliness. She became a guiding beacon, a pilot who guided me through the perilous waters ahead.

CHAPTER 8
IN PURSUIT OF PERFECTION

I didn't need the figures to know that I had become Gion Kobu's most popular maiko. I merely had to check my schedule. It was scheduled for a year and a half.

My calendar was so tight that a prospective customer had to confirm any tentative booking a month before the engagement, and, while I always kept a couple of slots open for emergencies, they were always filled a week in advance. If I had a few minutes available in my evening schedule, I would book them on my way home from the Nyokoba, promising five minutes here and ten minutes there. While I ate lunch, I had Kuniko write down these extra jobs in my appointment ledger.

Basically, I was booked solid for the entire five years that I worked as a maiko. I worked seven days a week, 365 days a year, from the age of fifteen to twenty-one. I have never taken a day off. I worked every Saturday and Sunday. I worked both New Year's Eve and New Year's Day.

I was the only person in the Iwasaki okiya who didn't take a day off during this time, and I could have been the only one in Gion Kobu as well. At the very least, it was better than not functioning.

I wasn't sure how to have fun. When I had some free time, I would go out with friends, but being in public was stressful for me.

The moment I stepped outside the door, I became "Mineko of Gion Kobu." Admirers mobbed me wherever I went, and I felt forced to play the part. I was constantly on. If someone wanted to take a photo with me, I allowed them. If someone requested an autograph, I gave it to her. It never stopped.

I was concerned that if I didn't keep the professional demeanor of a maiko at all times, I'd come apart. In fact, I was much better at home alone, thinking my own ideas, reading a book, or listening to music. That was the only way I could completely relax.

It's difficult to picture living in a society where everyone—your friends, sisters, and even your mother—is a rival. I found it quite disorienting. I couldn't tell the difference between friend and adversary; I had no idea who or what to believe. All of this eventually took its toll on my mental health, and I began to suffer from emotional problems. I had occasional nervousness, insomnia, and difficulties speaking.

I was worried that if I didn't loosen up, I'd become sick. So I resolved to become funny. I bought many recordings of funny stories and listened to them every day. I created my own tiny routines and tested them out at ozashiki. I pretended the banquet room was a playground and that I was there to have fun.

It really helped. I started to feel better and was able to focus more on what was going on in the room. Dance and other art forms can be taught, but the technique for making an ozashiki glitter cannot. This requires a specific ability and years of experience.

Every ozashiki is unique, even within the same ochaya. The arrangement of the room reveals a lot about the guests' class. How valuable is the scroll that hangs in the tokonoma? Which dishes are on the table? Where is the food from? A trained geiko understands these nuances the moment she enters an ozashiki and adjusts her behavior accordingly. My parents' aesthetic training helped me get started in this path.

Next, we must understand how to steer the entertainment. Does the host enjoy watching dances, having smart conversations, or playing funny games? When we get to know a consumer, we memorize his or her unique preferences and dislikes so that we can better serve him in the future.

Ochaya are not just utilized for entertainment. They also serve as forums for critical corporate and political conversations. An ozashiki creates a private environment in which participants know they will be comfortable and their privacy will be respected.

Auntie Oima explained that the reason our hair decorations have pointy ends is so that we can defend our customers from attacks. And that the coral ones worn in the cooler months can be used to evaluate the safety of the sake because coral breaks apart in the presence of toxins.

Sometimes the most valuable service a geiko can do is to blend into the wall and become invisible. If suitable, she will position herself at the room's entrance and use a little signal to alert the host when someone approaches. Alternatively, if asked, she will inform anyone approaching that the visitors do not want to be bothered.

The sake heater, also known as kanban, is one of the teahouse's specialties. The kanban fills a flask with sake before placing it in a pan of simmering water to reheat it. It sounds straightforward, yet each guest likes his or her sake served at a specific temperature. The okanagan's skill is to calculate how many degrees of heat will be lost while the sake goes from the kitchen to the banquet room, ensuring that the temperature is correct when it arrives. This is no little accomplishment. I liked the job of bringing sake because I enjoyed conversing with the kanban. They were always full of interesting behind-the-scenes details.

As I previously stated, teahouses tend to have multigenerational connections with their finest customers. One method the ochaya fosters this devotion is by recruiting their clients' offspring as temporary employees. Assistant Kanban is a popular post.

For example, a young guy starting college in Kyoto may apply for this job based on his father's recommendation in order to help him cover his expenditures. Everyone profits from this arrangement. The young man learns how the ochaya culture works from the inside out. He discovers how much care goes into even the smallest ozashiki and meets the local maiko and geiko. The father is helping to educate his son in the complex ways of the grownup world. And the ochaya is investing in a potential client.

I continued to give my dance classes my whole attention. Now that I was a professional dancer, I felt like I was finally making progress. So it came as a surprise when I got my second otome.

It occurred during rehearsals for the Yukatakai, the summer dances in which all Gion Kobu geikos take part. I was seventeen. We were practicing a group number. Big Mistress abruptly stopped the action, shouted my name, and instructed me to exit the stage. I could not believe it. I had not committed an error. The girl next to me did.

I confronted Mama Masako and yelled, "That's it. I am quitting! I received another otome, and this one was not my fault either!"

Mama Masako responded, calmly, "Fine." Go ahead. I mean, you didn't make any mistakes. How could she embarrass you in front of everyone? You, poor thing!"

She was encouraging me. Wow, she could see right through me. She knew I was always doing the opposite of what she ordered me to do.

"No, I mean it Mom, I'm really going to quit."

"It makes sense." It's precisely what I'd do if I were in your shoes."

"But if I quit, I would lose face. Maybe I should trick everyone and keep going. "I am not sure..."

"Well, that is another option…"

Just then, Yaeko entered the room. She had overheard our chat.

"You really did it this time, Mineko. "You have embarrassed us all."

She meant that my shame will result in a loss of face for every geiko from our bloodline.

But Mama Masako shoved her aside. "Yaeko, this is none of your business. Would you mind going into another room for a minute?"

Yaeko curved her lips into a faint smile. "Of course, this is my business. Her poor behavior makes me embarrassed as well."

Mama stated firmly, "Yae, don't be ridiculous. Could you please leave here?"

"Since when are you bossing me around?"

"This is between Mineko and myself. I want you to keep out of this."

"Well, if that's how you feel, I'm very sorry to bother you. Far be it from me to interfere with you and your 'beloved' Mineko. "Like she's worth it."

Yaeko stomped out of the room, but her words remained in my head. Maybe I was so horrible that I should just stop.

"Forgive me, Mama; I'm truly sorry. Maybe it's best if I give up."

"Whatever you decide to do is okay with me."

"But what if it's as Yaeko says?" What if I have brought shame on the house?"

"That is not a good enough argument. You mentioned it just a few minutes ago. If you quit, you may utterly lose face. If I were you, I would speak with the Big Mistress. See what she has to say. I bet she wants you to continue."

"Do you think so?" Thank you, mama. That is what I will do.

Mama Masako phoned Mother Sakaguchi, who arrived in a car.

As is customary, our contingent sat facing their contingent. Everyone bowed.

I waited for Mother Sakaguchi to defend my innocence.

"Mistress Aiko, I must express how grateful I am that you scolded Mineko in that manner. This is the kind of criticism she requires to become a genuine dancer. On her behalf, I sincerely request your continuing attention and direction.

As if on cue, the Iwasaki contingent bowed again. I was a heartbeat behind, just enough time to wonder, "What the heck is going on?" Then I received it. in a flash. Big Mistress was trying me again. Using the otome to propel myself ahead. She wanted me to know that the most important thing was to keep dancing. An occasional scolding was insignificant in comparison to what I could achieve or lose. My attitude and schoolgirl superiority had no place in any of this. And then something changed. I began to see the wider picture. I felt a renewed sense of devotion to what I was doing. I became a dancer.

I'm not sure what Mama Masako told Mother Sakaguchi when she called, how Mother Sakaguchi reacted, or what Mother Sakaguchi said to Mistress Aiko before we all met. Mother Sakaguchi, however, was conveying an important message to me through her expressive demonstration of humility. She was demonstrating how professionals dealt with their disputes in a non-reactive and helpful manner for all involved. I'd seen innumerable examples of this before, but I'd never fully comprehended it until that moment. I was really proud of Mother Sakaguchi's superb handling of the situation. Big Mistress may have scolded me initially, but Mother Sakaguchi taught me the actual lesson.

I still had a long way to go before becoming an adult, but I knew I wanted to be as excellent as the women in that room. Big Mistress thanked Madame Sakaguchi for her visit and, with her crew in tow, led Mother Sakaguchi to the entryway to say goodbye.

Right before she got into the car, Mother Sakaguchi bent down and whispered quietly into my ear:

"Mine-chan, work hard."

"Yes, I promise."

When we returned home, I went around the okiya and hauled in all the mirrors I could find for my room. I put them around the walls so that I could see myself from all sides and began to dance. From then on, I practiced like a madwoman. I changed into dance attire as soon as I stepped into the house at night and practiced until my eyes couldn't stay open any longer. Some nights, I only received an hour of sleep.

I examined myself as critically as I could. I attempted to analyze every detail of my actions and perfect every gesture. But there was something missing. Some form of expressiveness. I gave it some serious thinking. What might it be? Finally, it occurred to me that the problem was emotional, not physical.

The difficulty was that I had never fallen in love. My dance lacked the depth of feeling that comes from romantic desire. How could I convey genuine affection or loss if I didn't know them?

This knowledge was terrifying because everytime I thought of physical love, I remembered the moment my nephew attempted to rape me, and my mind stopped working. I was still immersed in the fear of the event. I was concerned there was something severely wrong with me. Was I so scared that I'd never be able to have a regular relationship? And this wasn't the only thing standing between me and intimacy. There was something deeper, possibly more sinister.

The truth is that I didn't like people. I hadn't when I was a little girl, and I still don't. My dislike for other people hampered me professionally as well as personally. It was my greatest weakness as a maiko. But I had no choice. I had to push myself to pretend I liked everybody.

When I look back and see this image of myself, this unworldly young woman, trying so hard to please yet refusing to let anyone near, it brings me to tears.

Most teenagers find the connection between the sexes perplexing, but I was completely lost. I had so little experience with men and boys that I lacked an intuitive sense of how to express warmth without inviting closeness. It was critical that I be pleasant with everyone. But if I was too friendly, the consumer would get the incorrect impression, which I didn't want to happen. It took me years to figure out how to strike a balance between pleasing men and keeping them away. I made several blunders at first since I didn't know how to give the proper signals.

One time, a very rich young man told me, "I'm going to study overseas. I'd like you to join me. Are there any objections?"

I was astounded. He presented his plans for me as if they were already finalized. I wasn't sure what to say.

Men who comprehend Gion Kobu's unspoken rules rarely break them. However, a naive individual like this one may misread my benevolence and take it too personally. I was left with no choice except to confront him directly. I explained to him that I was only doing my job and that, while I thought he was a good man, I had not intended to give him the impression that I was interested in him.

Another occasion, a young client gave me an expensive doll from his homeland. He was so anxious to give me the present that he couldn't wait for his next ozashiki. He brought it to the okiya and knocked on its door.

This was a clear breach of decorum, yet I felt sad for him, even if it was disturbing. I couldn't believe he thought he had the right to come into my home. I still attempted to be courteous.

"Thank you anyhow, although I'm not much into dolls. Please give it to someone else who would appreciate it."

A story quickly circulated among my regular customers that I detested dolls.

When I was on assignment in Tokyo, my client led me to a shop specializing in name-brand luxury things.

"Pick out anything you want," he continued.

I rarely received gifts from clients, so I rejected and stated I was content to browse around. I noticed a watch I liked and subconsciously said, "Nice watch." The next day, the client had the watch brought to my hotel. I promptly returned it. It served as an excellent reminder to keep my guard up at all times.

These episodes occurred when I was sixteen or seventeen, and they demonstrate my immaturity and inexperience. They indicate how much I still needed to learn.

Sometimes my innocence resulted in genuine embarrassment.

The first New Year after becoming a maiko, I was invited to attend the Hatsugama (first tea ceremony of the year) at the Urasenke Tea School, Japan's preeminent stronghold of aesthetic accuracy. It was an honor to be invited, and I behaved appropriately in front of the elite audience.

Geiko study the tea ceremony to absorb the graciousness it brings, but we must also be prepared to execute it publicly during the yearly Miyako Odori event.

The Kaburenjo has a massive tearoom that can accommodate up to 300 guests. On her assigned day, a geiko performs the ceremony five times, at fifteen-minute intervals, to accommodate the 1,450 audience members. She solely makes tea for the two persons who have been invited to attend as guests of honor. The remaining 298 persons are served by women who have made tea in an anteroom. Every geiko must study tea, hence there is a close tie between the Urasenke Tea School and the Gion Kobu.

We were sitting in a long row around a large room at the Hatsugama when an attendant began passing an interesting-looking cup from visitor to guest. The cup had a pointed stem but no base, similar to a golf tee or mushroom. There was no way to set the cup down. You had to drink whatever was in there. "What fun," I thought, and when it came to me, I downed the contents in one gulp.

It was horrible. I'd never tasted anything so bad. I thought I'd throw up. Mrs. Kayoko Sen, the wife of the former director of the Urasenke Tea School, who was usually extremely polite to me, chuckled and said, "What's the matter Mine-chan?" Don't you enjoy sake?"

SAKE? At first, I grimaced. And then I panicked. I'd just breached the law! Oh my God, what if I was arrested? My father instilled such fear of the law in me that I was scared of committing crimes. What will I do now? But then the cup came back around my way, and nobody seemed to notice anything was odd. I didn't want to cause a scene in front of all these important people, so I held my breath and swallowed it again. By the end of the celebration, I had consumed a large amount of sake.

I started feeling funny, but I was able to complete my dance without incident. I attended my regular number of banquets in the evening and made it through them as well. But when I got home and walked into the vestibule of the okiya, I fell flat on my face. Everyone in the okiya made a huge deal as they helped me remove my outfit and get into my futon.

The next day, I awoke at 6 a.m. As usual, I was overtaken by a strong sense of guilt and self-loathing. What did I do last night? I couldn't remember what happened after I left the tea school. I couldn't recall anything from any of the ozashiki I'd attended.

I wanted to crawl into a hole and die, but I had to get up for class. Not only had I disobeyed the law, but I may have also acted disgracefully. It was almost too much to handle. I did not want to face anyone.

I forced myself to get up and attend class. I took my class with Big Mistress, but I was convinced that everyone was staring at me strangely. I was quite uncomfortable. I sought to be excused from the remainder of my classes and returned to the okiya. As soon as I got through the door, I headed straight to the closet. I rocked myself and murmured, "I apologize. Excuse me. "I'll never do it again," I told myself as a mantra.

I hadn't spent that much time in the closet in a long time, and I stayed there all afternoon. I finally came out when it was time to get ready for work.

This was the last time I indulged in the comforts of my boyhood shelter. I never went back in the closet again.

I wonder why I was so harsh on myself. It was something about my father, something about feeling so isolated. I was certain that self-discipline was the solution to all problems.

I believed that self-discipline was essential to beauty.

CHAPTER 9
TOSHIO

His stage name was Shintaro Katsu. I met him when I was fifteen, during one of the first ozashiki I went to after becoming a maiko. He had asked one of the older maiko to invite me to come over so he could meet me.

She introduced him as Toshio. Toshio was Japan's biggest movie star. I knew his name, but I rarely went to the movies and didn't know his face. Anyway, I was not impressed. He was dressed as a slob. He was dressed in a yukata (cotton kimono), which is too casual for an ozashiki and was somewhat rumpled. He still wore pancake makeup on his neck.

I was only in the ozashiki for approximately five minutes and did not speak with him directly. I remember thinking, "What an unsavory person." I hoped he wouldn't ask for me again.

A few days later, I went by the ochaya on my way home from school. I ran across Toshio, who was with his wife, and he introduced me to her. She is a famous actress, and I was delighted to meet her.

Toshio visited Gion Kobu almost every night. In fact, he asked for me several times. I denied as much as possible, but karyukai politeness required that I appear occasionally. I had expressly begged the okasan of the ochaya to keep me away from him, but she could only do so much. It was business, after all, and the okasan needed to accommodate her clients' reasonable wishes.

Toshio once asked the accompanist if he might borrow her shamisen for a minute. She handed it to him, and he began to play the ballad Nagare ("flowing"). I could not believe it! He was extremely talented. I felt goosebumps all around.

"Where did you learn to play like that?" I asked him. It was the first genuine thing I had ever said to him.

"Actually, my father is the iemoto of the Kineya School of shamisen balladry and I have been playing since I was a little boy."

"I'm extremely impressed. What additional secrets are you keeping?"

The scales slipped from my eyes, and I saw him in a completely new light. There was more than meets the eye.

For fun, I told him that I would only come to his ozashiki if he played the shamisen for me there. It was an impertinent request on my side, but from then on, anytime I joined an ozashiki he was hosting, there was a shamisen ready to go. Things went on like this for three years. He kept asking for me, and I went just sometimes, usually to hear him perform.

One night, when I was eighteen, I was taking sake from the kitchen to an ozashiki. I was going to climb up the stairs to the second floor when I noticed him coming down them. I was ashamed to be caught so publicly because I had declined to join his ozashiki that evening. He ran down the stairs and grabbed the tray from my grasp.

"Mineko, come here in a minute," he urged, pushing me into one of the maid's chambers.

Before I knew it, he wrapped his arms around me and kissed me on the lips.

"Yeech, stop." I struggled free. "The only person allowed to do that is Big John, my dog."

This was my first kiss. And I did not find it enticing at all. I thought I was experiencing an allergic response. I developed goosebumps, my hair stood on end, and I came out in a cold sweat. After overcoming astonishment and panic, I rapidly developed a burning rage.

"How dare you!""I hissed. "Don't touch me ever again. Ever!"

"Oh, Mine-chan, don't you like me even slightly?"

"Like? What do you mean by "like"? Love has nothing to do with it!"

I'm embarrassed to confess that now, but even at the age of eighteen, I felt that kissing could cause pregnancy. I was terrified to death.

I stormed into the office and told the okasan everything. "I don't want to see him again. No matter how often he asks for me. "He's disgusting, and his demeanor is despicable."

She informed me that I was overreacting.

"Mine-chan, you need to grow up a little here. It was an innocent kiss. It's nothing to get so worked up about. He's an important customer, and I'd like you to allow him some leeway."

She allayed my anxieties and, over the next few weeks, persuaded me that it was okay to accept one of his persistent demands for an appearance.

I entered the ozashiki with doubts, but Toshio was obviously contrite. He swore not to put his finger on me. I resumed my habit of honoring one out of every five of his requests.

One evening, he requested playfully, "I know I'm not supposed to touch you, but could you place one of your fingers on my knee? In exchange for all my efforts on the shamisen?"

I pretended to be handling something infected and gently placed the tip of my index finger on the top of his knee. It was like a game.

After three months with the index finger, he asked, "How about three fingers?"

Then, "How about five fingers?"

And afterward, "What about your entire palm?""

Then one night, he became serious. "Mineko, I think I'm falling in love with you."

I was too inexperienced to distinguish between flirting and the genuine thing. I assumed he was fooling around.

"Oh, Toshio-san, how can that be? Aren't you married? I am not interested in married men. Besides, if you're married, you're already in love!"

"That isn't necessarily true, Mineko. "Love and marriage do not always go together."

"Well, I don't know. However, you should not be fooling around like this, even if you are joking. Your wife would be devastated if she heard, and I'm sure you would never want to hurt her. Or your children. "Your primary responsibility is to make them happy."

My father was the only adult male I ever knew. All of my beliefs about love and responsibility came from him.

"Mineko, I did not want this to happen. "It just did."

"Well, there is nothing we can do about it so you better forget about the whole thing right now."

"So, how do you propose I do that?"

"I have no idea." It is not my problem. But I am confident you will do just fine. Anyway, you are not who I am looking for. I'm looking for a great passion, someone who will sweep me off my feet and teach me everything about love. And then I'm going to become an excellent dancer."

"What is he like, this great passion of yours?""

"I don't know because I haven't discovered him yet. But I do know a few things about him. He isn't married. He is well-versed in art, so I can discuss my work with him. He will never try to get me to stop dancing. And he is really intelligent, as I have many questions. I believe he is a professional of some sort.

I shouted out my entire laundry list of requirements. I obviously had in mind someone as intelligent as my father or Dr. Tanigawa.

Toshio-san seemed disappointed.

"But what about me?""

"How about you?""

Do I have a chance?"

"It doesn't sound like that, does it?"

"So you're saying you don't really like me. Is this it?"

"Yes, I like you. But I am talking about something different. I am talking about the love of my life."

"What if I get divorced?""

"That's not an answer." "I don't want to hurt anyone."

"But my wife and I are not in love with each other."

"Then, why did you marry?"

"She was in love with someone else." I took that as a challenge and chose to steal her away from him."

Now I was becoming annoyed.

"That's the stupidest thing I've ever heard."

"I understand. "You can see why I want a divorce."

"How about your children?" "I could never love someone who treated his children that way."

Toshio was twice the age I was. But as we talked, I felt more like an adult.

"I don't think we should discuss this any more. We are just going around in circles. "This discussion is over."

"I apologize, Mineko, but I refuse to give up. I'm going to keep trying.

I decided to put down my own challenge. I believed if I played hard to get, he'd become tired of the game and forget about me.

"If you truly love me, I want you to show it. Remember the poet Onono Komachi? How did she have Officer Fukakusa visit her for 100 nights before giving him her hand? So, I want you to go to Gion Kobu every night for the next three years. Every night. Without exception. Most of the time, I will not attend your ozashiki, but I will always check to see if you arrived. If you finish this challenge, we can talk again.

I never believed he'd actually do it.

But he did. He visited Gion Kobu every night for the next three years, including big holidays such as New Year's Day. And he always demanded that I attend his ozashiki. This I did once or twice per week. Throughout these years, we formed a really civilized friendship. I danced. He played the shamisen. We mostly spoke about art.

Toshio was an extremely talented man. His upbringing had given him a solid foundation in the aesthetic ideals that I was attempting to perfect. He turned out to be a pleasant and vivacious teacher, and once he began to take me seriously, he was the ultimate gentleman. He never crossed the line of propriety again, and I no longer felt sexually threatened in his company. In fact, he became one of my favorite clients.

Meanwhile, I was gradually and steadily falling under his spell. I eventually realized that I was feeling something for him that I hadn't felt for anyone else. I wasn't sure what it was, but I had a strong sense it was sexual desire. It was an attraction. I felt attracted to him. This was what everyone was talking about.

This is where we were when he asked my friend to bring the bouquet of cosmos to my bedside. It was his charming way of keeping his commitment to visit me every day.

When I discovered the flowers were from Toshio, I became emotional. I wasn't sure if this was love. But it was certainly something. I felt a tightness in my chest whenever I thought about him, which was all the time. It made me feel shy and awkward. I wanted to talk to him about what was going on, but I wasn't sure what to say. I believe the small door in my heart was beginning to crack open. And I fought it every step of the way.

After 10 days, I felt good enough to dance again. I was still unable to speak, but Mama proclaimed that I was available to entertain and summoned the dresser.

I produced a bunch of note cards with short lines like "How nice to see you," "It's been a long time," "Thank you, I'm fine," "I'd love to dance," and "Everything is working except my voice." I used the cards to get through 10 days of ozashiki. It was enjoyable, actually. The cards and pantomime brought a touch of humor to the ozashiki, which the visitors seemed to appreciate.

It took ten days for my throat soreness to subside. Finally, I was able to swallow comfortably. My kidney returned from its vacation and began to operate normally again. I felt better.

The most unsettling side effect of the journey was the amount of weight I lost. I was down to 86 pounds. As previously stated, the entire maiko ensemble weighs 30 to 40 pounds, so you can imagine how tough it was for me to move around and dance while in costume. But I was so thrilled to be up and about that I persevered and ate everything I could. If I couldn't bear the weight of the kimono, I couldn't work.

Despite my weakness, I was able to do a lot during this time due to the abundance of activities. I appeared on stage several times at Exposition Plaza. I appeared in a film directed by Kon Ichikawa (and written by Zenzo Matsuyama, one of my very first customers). The movie was shown at Kyoto's government Monopoly Theater, but I was too busy to see it.

I WAS UNWORLDLY IN MANY WAYS, but as an adult, I felt compelled to leave the okiya and try to live independently. I told Mama. She was doubtful but didn't try to stop me. "That's an intriguing notion. You are welcome to try, but I doubt you will be able to handle it.

In February 1971, when I was twenty-one, I rented a huge flat on Kitashirakawa Ave. The rent was $1,100 per month, which was a large sum of money at the time. I hired pros to help me move in and decorate the place.

As soon as I moved in, one of my girlfriends paid me a visit.

"Mineko, this is fantastic." Congratulations."

Thank you, Mari. Could I offer you a cup of tea?"

"That would be lovely, thank you."

I felt quite grown up. I walked into the kitchen to make tea. I put water in the teakettle and placed it on top of the burner. But nothing occurred. The burner did not light. I was unsure what to do. I realized I'd never used a stove before.

"What is taking so long?" Mari stuck her head inside the kitchen.

"Oh, sorry," I replied. "The gas isn't coming out and the flame isn't lighting."

"That's because you have to do this," she added, turning on the burner.

I was quite impressed. It's like magic.

She continues to repeat this story now. It still gets a good laugh.

One day, I decided to clean the apartment and took the vacuum from the cupboard. I pushed it, but it did not begin to move. I believed it was broken and called home. Our appliance technician came rushing over to investigate what was wrong. He quickly assessed the situation.

"Mine-chan, the thing about electrical appliances is that you have to take the plug and stick it into an outlet or they won't work."

"You mean it's not broken?""

Even I felt ashamed about that one.

Next, I decided to make supper. First, the rice. I had previously visited the rice shop and placed my order. I walked to the beautiful new rice canister on top of the counter and opened it. However, there was nothing inside! I called home.

"My order from Tomiya's did not arrive. Did you forget to pay your bill?"

Mama called the shop, and the proprietor, with whom we had been doing business for years, arrived immediately.

As soon as I saw him, I began to complain.

"Seriously, Gramps. You shouldn't tease me like this. "I really need my order."

"It is sitting right here in the entranceway. In this bag. The one with "rice" on it.

"But why isn't it inside the container? I removed the cover, and it was empty.

"Mine-chan, my job is to deliver rice to your door. You are expected to place it in the container yourself."

Before moving, I went to a large department store and charged everything I needed to the okoya's account, including furniture, bedding, cooking utensils, and dishes. I never looked at the price tag for anything. Mama was shocked when she saw the invoices, but she paid them anyway.

We used to pay for little items in cash back then, before credit cards. I couldn't charge for groceries. I'd have to go shopping for these myself. As a result, Mama provided me with an allowance for incidentals. "You'll need money for food," she continued, passing me $5,000. I put the money in my handbag and went out to buy in the neighborhood. I located the butcher, grocer, and seafood store. I didn't know how much anything cost, but I assumed I had enough to acquire what I wanted.

The first place I visited was a vegetable store. I purchased potatoes, carrots, and a daikon radish. I took off a ten thousand-yen note ($100) and handed it to the merchant. My heartbeat was racing. It was the first time I had given someone real money to pay for something.

After paying the bill, I scooped up my things and proudly exited the store. But the shopkeeper ran after me, yelling something. I was convinced I had made a huge mistake and began apologizing profusely, "I'm so sorry. I'm simply not used to this. I didn't mean to make the mistake. Please forgive me."

The man must have thought I had lost my wits.

"I don't understand what you're talking about, Miss. "But you forgot your change."

"Change? What changes?"

"Here's your change, Miss. I apologize, but please take it. I'm busy. "I do not have time for these games."

And that is how I learned about change.

Now I was truly shopping!

Returning home, full of accomplishment, I decided to prepare supper. The first item I made was a large pot of nikujaga, a beef and potato stew. I cooked plenty for ten people. It took me from lunchtime till four o'clock. When I believed it was finished, I wrapped it up, called a cab, and carefully transported it to the okiya.

"I've cooked something for you all," I happily proclaimed. "Come, eat, and enjoy!"

My family obediently sat around the table, sampling the food. They each took a spoonful and looked at each other. Nobody said anything, and nobody was chewing.

Finally, Kuniko spoke up. "It's not bad for your first try."

Mama and Auntie Taji were glancing at their plates. They still had not said anything. I was persistent.

"Enjoy and be grateful for anything you're served. Isn't this what the Buddha taught? Isn't it?"

Her response was: "That's true, but everything has its limits."

"What does that mean exactly?"

"Mineko, did you try this before presenting it to us?"

"I did not have to. I could tell it was wonderful by how it smelled.

Shows you what I knew about cooking.

"Here. "You take a bite."

It was the oddest thing I'd ever tasted. I was quite impressed with myself for creating something so bizarre.

My first impulse was to spit it out, but I refrained. If the others had managed to eat one or two mouthfuls, I would have as well. I remembered my father's maxim, "The samurai betrays no weakness when starving." But this time, I amended it to "The samurai betrays no weakness when eating," and swallowed hard.

Standing up, I remarked, "It could use more work," and began to leave.

"What will we do with the leftovers?""Kuniko called after me."

"Throw them out," I replied, hurrying to the door.

My prospects for independent living did not appear promising.

I came to the okiya every day to get ready for work. Mama kept inquiring when she would meet my beau. I still hadn't spent any time with Toshio outside of the ochaya, but our three-year contract was up in May. I felt I'd best get her viewpoint. I made arrangements to introduce them.

If I reminded her once, I reminded her 100 times. "Promise me you will dress as simply as possible."

She appeared to be heading to a wedding. She wore a formal black kimono.

"Mom! What are you doing wearing that outfit? After you promised! "Please return to your room and change into something simpler."

"But why?" Do you want me to look well when I meet your friend?"

"Just change. Please."

"Into what?"

"Any old thing will do."

"I do not understand you, Mineko. "Most girls want their mothers to look beautiful."

"Well, I don't." "Especially if you're prettier than I am."

We were shooting at each other before we left the house.

We met at Toshio's traditional ochaya.

It did not go well. I was completely insane. Thinking of Toshio as a customer was one thing. Thinking of him as my boyfriend was a very different thing. I felt extremely self-conscious. I couldn't think of what to say. I was flushed from head to toe, and my mind was as blank as a white piece of paper. It was agonizing.

CHAPTER 10
LESSONS OF THE HEART

I was unworldly in many ways, but as an adult, I felt compelled to leave the okiya and try to live independently. I told Mama. She was doubtful but didn't try to stop me. "That's an intriguing notion. You are welcome to try, but I doubt you will be able to handle it.

In February 1971, when I was twenty-one, I rented a huge flat on Kitashirakawa Ave. The rent was $1,100 per month, which was a large sum of money at the time. I hired pros to help me move in and decorate the place.

As soon as I moved in, one of my girlfriends paid me a visit.

"Mineko, this is fantastic." Congratulations."

Thank you, Mari. Could I offer you a cup of tea?"

"That would be lovely, thank you."

I felt quite grown up. I walked into the kitchen to make tea. I put water in the teakettle and placed it on top of the burner. But nothing occurred. The burner did not light. I was unsure what to do. I realized I'd never used a stove before.

"What is taking so long?" Mari stuck her head inside the kitchen.

"Oh, sorry," I replied. "The gas isn't coming out and the flame isn't lighting."

"That's because you have to do this," she added, turning on the burner.

I was quite impressed. It's like magic.

She continues to repeat this story now. It still gets a good laugh.

One day, I decided to clean the apartment and took the vacuum from the cupboard. I pushed it, but it did not begin to move. I believed it was broken and called home. Our appliance technician came rushing over to investigate what was wrong. He quickly assessed the situation.

"Mine-chan, the thing about electrical appliances is that you have to take the plug and stick it into an outlet or they won't work."

"You mean it's not broken?""

Even I felt ashamed about that one.

Next, I decided to make supper. First, the rice. I had previously visited the rice shop and placed my order. I walked to the beautiful new rice canister on top of the counter and opened it. However, there was nothing inside! I called home.

"My order from Tomiya's did not arrive. Did you forget to pay your bill?"

Mama called the shop, and the proprietor, with whom we had been doing business for years, arrived immediately.

As soon as I saw him, I began to complain.

"Seriously, Gramps. You shouldn't tease me like this. "I really need my order."

"It is sitting right here in the entranceway. In this bag. The one with "rice" on it.

"But why isn't it inside the container? I removed the cover, and it was empty.

"Mine-chan, my job is to deliver rice to your door. You are expected to place it in the container yourself."

Before moving, I went to a large department store and charged everything I needed to the okoya's account, including furniture, bedding, cooking utensils, and dishes. I never looked at the price tag for anything. Mama was shocked when she saw the invoices, but she paid them anyway.

We used to pay for little items in cash back then, before credit cards. I couldn't charge for groceries. I'd have to go shopping for these myself. As a result, Mama provided me with an allowance for incidentals. "You'll need money for food," she continued, passing me $5,000. I put the money in my handbag and went out to buy in the neighborhood. I located the butcher, grocer, and seafood store. I didn't know how much anything cost, but I assumed I had enough to acquire what I wanted.

The first place I visited was a vegetable store. I purchased potatoes, carrots, and a daikon radish. I took off a ten thousand-yen note ($100) and handed it to the merchant. My heartbeat was racing. It was the first time I had given someone real money to pay for something.

After paying the bill, I scooped up my things and proudly exited the store. But the shopkeeper ran after me, yelling something. I was convinced I had made a huge mistake and began apologizing profusely, "I'm so sorry. I'm simply not used to this. I didn't mean to make the mistake. "Please forgive me."

The man must have thought I had lost my wits.

"I don't understand what you're talking about, Miss. "But you forgot your change."

"Change? What changes?"

"Here's your change, Miss. I apologize, but please take it. I'm busy.

"I do not have time for these games."

And that is how I learned about change.

Now I was truly shopping!

Returning home, full of accomplishment, I decided to prepare supper. The first item I made was a large pot of nikujaga, a beef and potato stew. I cooked plenty for ten people. It took me from lunchtime till four o'clock. When I believed it was finished, I wrapped it up, called a cab, and carefully transported it to the okiya.

"I've cooked something for you all," I happily proclaimed. "Come, eat, and enjoy!"

My family obediently sat around the table, sampling the food. They each took a spoonful and looked at each other. Nobody said anything, and nobody was chewing.

Finally, Kuniko spoke up. "It's not bad for your first try."

Mama and Auntie Taji were glancing at their plates. They still had not said anything. I was persistent.

"Enjoy and be grateful for anything you're served. Isn't this what the Buddha taught? Isn't it?"

Her response was: "That's true, but everything has its limits."

"What does that mean exactly?"

"Mineko, did you try this before presenting it to us?"

"I did not have to. I could tell it was wonderful by how it smelled.

Shows you what I knew about cooking.

"Here. "You take a bite."

It was the oddest thing I'd ever tasted. I was quite impressed with myself for creating something so bizarre.

My first impulse was to spit it out, but I refrained. If the others had managed to eat one or two mouthfuls, I would have as well. I remembered my father's maxim, "The samurai betrays no weakness when starving." But this time, I amended it to "The samurai betrays no weakness when eating," and swallowed hard.

Standing up, I remarked, "It could use more work," and began to leave.

"What will we do with the leftovers?""Kuniko called after me."

"Throw them out," I replied, hurrying to the door.

My prospects for independent living did not appear promising.

I came to the okiya every day to get ready for work. Mama kept inquiring when she would meet my beau. I still hadn't spent any time with Toshio outside of the ochaya, but our three-year contract was up in May. I felt I'd best get her viewpoint. I made arrangements to introduce them.

If I reminded her once, I reminded her 100 times. "Promise me you will dress as simply as possible."

She appeared to be heading to a wedding. She wore a formal black kimono.

"Mom! What are you doing wearing that outfit? After you promised! "Please return to your room and change into something simpler."

"But why?" Do you want me to look well when I meet your friend?"

"Just change. Please."

"Into what?"

"Any old thing will do."

"I do not understand you, Mineko. "Most girls want their mothers to look beautiful."

"Well, I don't." "Especially if you're prettier than I am."

We were shooting at each other before we left the house.

We met at Toshio's traditional ochaya.

It did not go well. I was completely insane. Thinking of Toshio as a customer was one thing. Thinking of him as my boyfriend was a very different thing. I felt extremely self-conscious. I couldn't think of what to say. I was flushed from head to toe, and my mind was as blank as a white piece of paper. It was agonizing.

My hand shook as I approached to offer the sake. My professional demeanor had entirely evaporated. When we arrived home, Mama teased me cruelly. "Mine-chan, I have never seen you so tense. It was a riot, everybody. Our calm princess was flushing from the roots of her hair. She was trembling so severely that she could hardly pour the sake. She had nothing to say. This is great. I guess I've finally discovered your weakness."

I knew from the beginning that introducing them would be a mistake.

On May 23, 1971, three years to the day I issued my challenge, I received a telegram from Toshio via the okasan of his ochaya inviting me to meet him at the Ishibei Koji Inn. The mail stated that I did not need to attend dressed in costume. This indicated that it was a private meeting, not an ozashiki. Plus, it was midday.

So I wore a modest kimono made of black Oshima pongee with red roses and a red and white obi embroidered with black maple leaves.

When I arrived at the inn, Toshio was playing mahjong with some of his buddies. The game was soon over, and the other players left.

Except for that one clandestine kiss, I'd never been alone in a room with him before.

He got right to the point.

"I've been to see you every night for the past three years, just as you requested. Now I'd like to chat about us. Do I have a chance? What are your thoughts?"

I was not thinking. I was feeling. I was aware that he had a wife and children, but it did not appear to matter at the time. I could not help myself. I responded honestly.

"I am not sure. I mean, this had never occurred to me before. But I think I am in love with you."

"In that case," the man replied, "I think we should make the proper arrangements so that we can be together."

I lowered my eyes and silently nodded yes. We got up and walked straight to the okasan of the ochaya. She listened as he described the problem. I don't think she was surprised by what he said.

"Toshio-san, you are one of my most valued customers," she said. "And you two seem to genuinely care for each other. For these reasons, I accept participation in this conversation. However, everything must pass through the proper channels. If you wish to be with Mineko, you must first get permission from her family.

I knew the rules. I was so agitated that I had forgotten about them.

The "flower and willow world" is a distinct society with its own set of rules and regulations, as well as ceremonies and rituals. It permits for sexual relationships outside of marriage, but only if they follow certain standards.

The majority of long-term partnerships in Japan, such as those between man and wife and teacher and disciple, are arranged by a third party who continues to operate as a go-between even after the two have been united. Mother Sakaguchi so arranged for my apprenticeship with the iemoto and stayed available to intercede whenever a difficulty arose. When the ochaya's okasan consented to be a "party to the discussion," she essentially accepted the role of our go-between. We immediately hurried to the okiya to consult with Mama, as she had advised.

"I believe that people who love each other should be together," she exclaimed, ever the romantic.

Toshio promised Mama Masako that he would divorce his wife.

Mama Masako granted us her blessing.

I canceled all of my appointments for the remainder of the day due to illness and returned to the inn with Toshio. We went into his room. Neither of us spoke much at first. We simply sat there, taking in each other's company. Finally, we started speaking in bits and pieces. Our conversation naturally drifted to aesthetics. The day eventually faded into the evening.

Dinner was served to us in our room by a maid. I could hardly swallow anything. The maid returned and informed us that the bath was ready. I rejected because I had already washed twice that day, once when I woke up in the morning and once before getting prepared to see Toshio.

I hadn't planned on staying the night, so I was shocked when the maid spread out two sets of futons side by side. I didn't know what to do, so I continued chatting. Knowing his insatiable passion in the arts, I introduced one topic after another: music, dance, and theater. Before I knew it, midnight had passed.

Toshio asked, "Mineko, don't you want to get some sleep?"

"Thanks," I answered as enthusiastically as I could, "but I don't sleep much. I am still wide awake. Why don't you lie down and rest?"

I was straining to keep my eyes open, hoping that Toshio would fall asleep and save me from having to make a decision. He sprawled up on top of one of the futons without getting under the covers and continued to talk. I remained where I was, seated at the low table. Neither of us moved positions until the sky brightened.

I could not keep my head up any longer. I decided to stretch for a few minutes, but I promised myself I would not fall asleep. I carefully lay down on the second futon. I believed it was impolite to turn my back on Toshio, so I curled up like a shrimp. He asked me to come closer.

"I'm terribly sorry," I replied, "but I don't think I can do that."

So he made the first move. He inched closer. Then he wrapped his arms around me and drew me into a tight embrace. I laid straight as a board, but inside I was trembling and trying not to cry. We barely moved from that position till the sun rose.

"I have to get to class," I replied, getting up to depart, marking the end of our first night together.

Now that I was a full-fledged geiko, I started taking some time off, one week in February following the Setsubun vacation and another in the summer. That year, I planned to take a short trip to Gion Matsuri. Toshio had to travel to Brazil for work. We decided to take advantage of this unexpected opportunity and meet in New York City once he finished.

Toshio flew into Kennedy on his way back to Japan, and I caught a Pan Am flight to meet him there. He waited for me for six hours. Toshio was not used to waiting for anything, but he did have a history of having others wait for him. I half expected him not to be present when I arrived. But he was. I was pleased to see him waiting there as I came off the plane.

We visited the Waldorf-Astoria hotel. We ran across Elizabeth Taylor in the foyer while checking in and chatted briefly. But we couldn't wait to get up to the room and left as soon as it was appropriate.

I could not wait to be alone with him. The bellboy shut the door, and I turned to face Toshio. He quickly burst into tears. I'd never seen a mature man cry like that before.

"Oh my sweetheart, what has happened? What is wrong?"

"I've tried everything, but my wife won't give me a divorce. I do not know what else to do. It does not appear to matter what I do. "Or whatever I say."

Toshio sounded on the verge of despair. He spoke to me for hours. About his wife. About his children. Regarding his sadness over the entire scenario. I was too concerned with him to worry about myself. I couldn't tolerate seeing his misery, so I finally reached out to him. For the first time. I wrapped my arms around him and felt him completely sink into my hug. I assumed this great proximity was love. This is it.

I set two final requirements for our partnership.

"I'll stick with you as long as it takes to persuade her. But you must promise me two things. You will never conceal secrets from me or tell me lies. If you do, it is finished. No questions were asked. "You will go your way, and I will go mine."

He pledged, and I became his.

I was astounded by the power of the animal lust that we released in each other. I exposed myself to him with hunger, feeling no timidity or shame. The ghost of my nephew's assault was laid to rest on that bed.

When I looked down and saw the blood on the sheets, my heart jumped for delight. I had given Toshio my most precious treasure, and I had done so with love. In some ways, it was both of our first experiences. He informed me that he had never deflowered a virgin before. I felt indescribably happy.

That night, some of Toshio's fans hosted a reception for him. He was ready to leave before I was, so I told him to go ahead while I took a bath. I still needed to put on my eyeliner and kimono, so I said I'd be back in half an hour.

After my quick bath, I got out of the tub and went to open the bathroom door. The knob would not turn. It was broken. I tried pulling and pushing, but it wouldn't budge. I began knocking on the door. Toshio had already left, so there was no one else to hear me. I looked around, and lo and behold, there was a telephone by the mirror. I picked it up. There was no dial tone. I clicked the hook a couple of times. Still nothing. I couldn't believe both the doorknob and the phone were broken, especially at the Waldorf-Astoria.

I sat inside the restroom for three hours. I felt cold and unpleasant. Finally, I heard something inside the room. Toshio knocked on the door.

"What are you doing in there, Mineko?""

At least one of us remained calm!

He soon recognized the hysteria in my voice and found someone to answer the door. I was glad to see him. But I was too fatigued by the events of the day to go out. Poor Toshio! He had been so preoccupied at the party that he had lost count of time. He felt horrible. It was really cute. He was truly an extremely considerate individual. Aside from this minor event, we had a wonderful four days together in New York City.

I'd found what I was looking for. I was madly in love, and the intensity of our desire changed my life. More than anything else, it influenced my dance, which achieved the expressiveness I had been looking for for so long. Emotion seems to flow from my heart into every movement and gesture, making them richer and more powerful.

Toshio played a conscious and active involvement in this process. He was a severe critic. Our enthusiasm was founded on our commitment to artistic brilliance, which remained its wellspring until the end. We did not have the kind of relationship where we sat around cuddling and whispering sweet nothings into one other's ears.

Toshio had spent more time as an actor pushing the frontiers of self-expression than I had as a dancer. In this regard, he was clearly my senior. Despite our differences in fields, he was able and willing to provide me with detailed, clear advice.

The Inoue style is known for its ability to convey intense emotion through simple, delicate motions. Toshio recognized how to meet the form's most difficult difficulty. Whereas Big Mistress mentored me from within the paradigm, Toshio guided me from the outside.

When I passed a mirror, I would unconsciously move slightly. Toshio would stop me and ask, "Why don't you do it this way?" His comments were frequently well-considered. I'd stop whatever I was doing and, using his suggestion, rehearse the movement right there, over and over.

We were living as a couple but had to keep our affair hidden from everyone save our closest colleagues. He was still married. We never compromised our intimacy when we were out together in public.

This was challenging, so we traveled abroad whenever possible. We never had our photo taken together, even while we were vacationers at an exotic resort. (Except for the unusual one in the photo insert.)

In 1973, we went on another vacation in New York. This time, we stayed at the Hilton Hotel. Mr. R. A. Toshio hosted a party for us, and he introduced me as his fiancée. I was ecstatic; I was confident that it was just a matter of time before I became his wife. The press learned that I was having an affair with a celebrity, and the paparazzi pursued me for weeks. But the strange part is that they assumed I was seeing someone else; they got the wrong guy. Toshio had a large property in the suburbs of Kyoto and another in Tokyo, but he spent every night with me. My place became a "love nest."

He made himself at home. I soon discovered an unexpected side to Toshio's character. He was extraordinarily, obsessively clean. Given my housekeeping abilities, this was advantageous for both of us. When he had time off and was at home alone, he would clean the entire flat from top to bottom. He wiped down all of the surfaces, including the kitchen and bathroom, with a damp cloth and then a dry one, just as my mother had taught me to do, though my housekeeping efforts were usually limited to running the vacuum cleaner around the living room floor and swishing a dishrag on the coffee table.

In my defense, I was quite busy. My schedule was as packed as it had been while I lived at the okiya, but I also had to take care of my living space. I went to the okiya every day to prepare for work, but I no longer had a team of maids to clean up after me at home.

Most of the time, I was able to keep it together. But then Toshio would do something that put my skills to the test, such as filming a movie in a Kyoto studio. He began returning home late at night with around ten of his pals in tow. When I returned home following a long day at work, Toshio would ask, "What do we have for these people to eat?"

I'd combine whatever ingredients we had in the house in a large pot and cook them all together. My early attempts were not fantastic, but they improved over time. Toshio made sure everyone's glasses were full. Nobody ever went home hungry or thirsty. I came to like our spontaneous parties.

Toshio was endearingly kind and outgoing. He was excellent around the house and spoke fondly of his children. I couldn't understand why things weren't going well for him at home.

CHAPTER 11
TRADITION MEETS MODERNITY

In early May, the city of Hakata in Kyushu has an annual event known as Dontaku. Every year, I was invited to attend, and we would travel from Kyoto as a group. I always stayed at the same hotel, ate at the same restaurants, and hung out with my local geisha friends. I've always shared a room with my best buddy Yuriko.

Late one afternoon, she and I were conversing, and the topic of the silent trek came up. The "silent pilgrimage" takes place during the Gion Festival, but few people are aware of it. I had heard rumors that Yuriko went on a silent journey, and I wanted to know if they were real.

For over a thousand years, Kyoto has hosted the Gion Festival, which is regarded as one of Japan's three most important festivals. The festival begins at the end of June and runs until July 24, and it includes a number of Shinto ceremonies and rituals. On July 17, the local gods are welcomed to enter their sacred palanquins, known as omikoshi, and are led out into the town for the last week of the festival. In summary, the gods are carried on the shoulders of carriers from Yasaka Shrine's main dwelling down Shijo Street to their temporary shrines along Shinkyogoku Avenue. The quiet journey takes place over the course of a week.

"I'd like to join the pilgrimage, too. What should I do to get included?" I asked her.

"It is not something you join. It is something you decide to do on your own, in privacy. "But, if you really want your prayer to come true, they say you have to do it for three years in a row," she replied. "And you can't tell anyone else what you're doing. That is part of its potency. You must do it in silence. Keep your gaze lowered. Do not make eye contact with anyone else. Concentrate totally on what is buried in your heart. Keep your prayer in mind throughout the pilgrimage, as that is why you are there.

I was deeply moved by her description. Yuriko's features were highly different, unlike the average Japanese face. Her eyes were astonishingly gorgeous. They were big, with delicate brown cores. She didn't say exactly what I wanted to know, but her smile betrayed the truth.

I couldn't stop thinking about why Yuriko was on the journey. What did she desire so badly? I kept bringing it up anytime I had the opportunity, but she always managed to shift the conversation. Eventually, my persistence paid off, and she gave up. She started telling me her story.

This was the first time I'd heard anything about her childhood.

Yuriko informed me she was born in January 1943 in Suzushi, a town on the Japan Sea coast. Her father's family has been in the fishing industry for several generations. Her father also owned a profitable fish company. Her father used to pay frequent visits to Gion Kobu when he was younger.

Yuriko's mother died shortly after her birth. Before she was weaned, she was sent to live with other relatives. During the war, the military requisitioned her father's company and converted it into a munitions factory. But her father continued to fish. Following the war, he reopened his business, and everything was going well. But he did not bring his daughter home. She continues to be passed down from relative to relative.

As his circumstances improved, her father resumed his visits to Gion Kobu and his friendship with a particular geiko. She married him, becoming Yuriko's stepmother. Yuriko was finally able to return to her father's side, and a younger sister joined the family. I think that was the first time she felt the comfort and love of a loving family. However, her bliss was not to last long. Her father's company has gone bankrupt. He got desperate and, unable to find a way out, spent his days in a drunken haze before hanging himself in front of his baby daughter's innocent eyes.

Yuriko's stepmother was at a loss for what to do and farmed Yuriko back out to her deceased husband's family. The family who took her in treated her like a beast of burden, without even providing her with shoes. They eventually sold her to a "slave trader" (zegen, men who roamed the countryside buying girls to sell in the sex trade). (This practice was made illegal with the prohibition of prostitution in 1959.) She was sold to a business in Kyoto's Shimabara entertainment district.

Shimabara used to be a licensed quarter where women known as oiran and tayu (courtesans, or high-class prostitutes) worked, albeit they were also skilled in traditional skills. A young oiran also experienced a "mizuage" ceremony, butchers consisted of being ceremoniously deflowered by a patron who had paid well for the privilege. (This alternative definition of the word "mizuage" has caused some confusion regarding what it means to be a geisha. Tayu and Oiran were confined within the district till their indentured servitude ended.

Yuriko's stepmother discovered what had happened to her and promptly to the okasan of the Y okiya in Gion Kobu, pleading for her assistance. The proprietress contacted an otokoshi, who expertly facilitated her transition from Shimabara to the okiya. Yuriko refused to return to her stepmother, so the okiya consented to welcome her into their care.

This all happened when Yuriko was twelve years old.

Yuriko was a pleasant person who worked tirelessly on her lessons and rose to the position of top geiko in Gion Kobu. Whenever she talked about how much better her life was in Gion Kobu than it had been for the first twelve years, her gorgeous big brown eyes welled up with tears.

Two years later, when we returned to Hakata, she finally told me why she was undertaking the silent trip. She had been in love with a particular man for many years and wished to marry him. That's the cause. This is what she hoped for each summer on her lonely trip. Her mind was made up, and despite receiving numerous proposals from other guys, she utterly ignored them.

Unfortunately, for political reasons, her sweetheart married someone else, albeit they continued to be in a relationship. In May 1980, she was diagnosed with cancer. I'm not sure if he caused her illness, but her feelings for him grew greater as a result. As if in response to her pleas, he gently nursed her as she died. Unfortunately, his efforts were in vain, and she died on September 22, 1981, at the young age of 37. In my mind, I feel she still loves him and that it will last for a thousand years, if not eternity.

Setsubun is in the middle of February. It is a holiday that used to mark the start of spring on the traditional lunar calendar. We commemorate the event by throwing beans around the house to ward off evil spirits and bring in good luck.

In Gion Kobu, we celebrate Setsubun by dressing up in goofy costumes and having a good time. My buddies and I always chose costumes that were themed with the previous year's events. When the United States handed over control of Okinawa to Japan in 1972, we dressed in Okinawan folk costumes.

This group of friends and I were in the habit of utilizing the tips we earned at Setsubun gatherings to pay for a Hawaiian vacation. We visited nearly forty ozashiki, spending as little as three minutes apiece to maximize our tips. That night, we earned more than $30,000, enough to go in style.

It was my time to be the tour director. Aside from arranging the arrangements, I was in charge of all of our money and passports, which I carried in my purse as we departed Kyoto. We planned to spend the night in Tokyo before flying for Honolulu the next day.

Unfortunately, I left my purse in a taxi on our way to the hotel. My traveling companions were not very empathetic. They responded: "Oh, Mineko, it's just like you to do something like this." I was trying so hard to be responsible and was irritated by their behavior.

I needed to acquire us fresh money and passports by the next afternoon. I called one of my customers to explain my predicament. He graciously agreed to lend me $30,000 in cash. I requested him to bring it to the hotel the next morning. I was debating which of my government connections to contact for emergency passports when I received a call notifying me that a businessman had found my purse in the back of the taxi. The cab driver delivered it to a police station, where I picked it up the next morning in time to catch our flight. In the commotion, I failed to inform my customer that I no longer required the $30,000, and he came running in with it just as we were leaving.

Despite the rocky start, we had a great day. In the end, my buddies thanked me for being an excellent tour guide. On a sunset cruise, we took hula classes, and the teacher recognized us as dancers. She asked that we do anything for her. We had so much fun that we ended up teaching Inoue-style dancing classes on the boat for the next three days. Many of our customers were well-connected in Hawaii, and they organized fantastic dinners for us on Kauai and Oahu.

One day, the breeze gently blew Miss M.'s hair. I'd never realized how prominent her bald spot was. Then I took a closer look at my other two friends. And then at myself.

All four of us had large bald spots on the top of our crowns. This is a common problem produced by maiko hairstyles, which begin with tying the hair at the crown of the head. The mass is held in place using a bamboo strip that exerts continual pressure on the hair's roots. Our hair can stay up for five days at a time, and the rat irritates the scalp as well. When the scalp itches, we frequently scratch it with the pointed tip of a hair accessory, further damaging the hair at the root. After a few years, the spot ultimately goes bald.

"You know what?" I recommend it. "I believe that after we return to Japan and the Miyako Odori is completed, we should all check into a hospital together and have our bald spots treated. What are your thoughts? Shall we strike an agreement?"

They agreed to think about it.

We began rehearsal as soon as we returned to Kyoto. I had to prepare a solo piece as well as engage in group rehearsals, and I was requested to assist the younger dancers with their parts. We didn't have time to discuss the surgery again until after the Odori opened. Miss Y. claimed she was too terrified to have it done, but the other three of us agreed to go ahead. We left for Tokyo the day the Odori closed and stayed in a hospital near Benkei Bridge.

The procedure consists of snipping the bald skin and bringing the edges together to tighten it, much like a facelift. My incision was closed with a dozen tiny stitches. The scalp contains a large number of capillaries, and the operation was quite bloody, but effective. Except it hurt to laugh.

Our main concern was that we were stuck in the hospital for several days. Our Tokyo customers did their best to keep us entertained. They paid us a visit and delivered meals from the top restaurants in town. But it was April, and we were upbeat. We grew bored and started bickering, so I made up adventures to keep us entertained. One afternoon, we sneaked out to go shopping. Then we began to sneak out at night to our favorite restaurants, despite our bandages. We would sneak back into the hospital in the middle of the night. Another afternoon, we danced our way to the gas station down the street.

The head nurse was furious: "This is not a psychiatric facility. Stop acting like madwomen. And please stop clogging up all of our phone lines."

After about ten days, the doctor removed our stitches, and we were free to depart. I believe the nursing staff was pleased to see us leave. I wonder if Missy. still has a bald area. I believe she does.

I returned to Kyoto and quickly settled back into my routine with Toshio. I'd missed him. But suddenly, living on my own seemed like too much trouble. It was a huge hardship for me to prepare and cook meals, clean the house, do the laundry, and prepare the bath—all while keeping my work commitments. There was never sufficient time. I only slept a few hours per night as it was. I couldn't cut back on my nighttime obligations, so the only way I could find extra time was to reduce the amount of time I spent practicing. The issue was between becoming a great dancer and keeping the house clean. There was no contest.

I went to speak with Mama. "Mom, my cooking is not getting any better. And I don't have enough time to rehearse properly. "What do you think I should do?"

"Have you considered moving home?"

"I do not know. What do you think?"

"I think it's a good idea."

So, that was it. I moved back to Okinawa in June 1972. I'd learned that I could be independent, but I didn't have to be. Furthermore, Toshio and I had the ability to stay at a hotel anytime we desired, which we did frequently. I had grown up. I was a fully developed geiko. I knew how to get around in the world. I knew how to manage money and shop. And I was in love.

I'm glad I moved back home when I did since it allowed me to be present for Big John's final months. He died on October 6, 1972.

CHAPTER 12
PROMISES AND PRIDE

On May 6, 1973, I made a visit to my parents. It was only the third time I had been to the house since leaving it eighteen years ago.

I'd heard my father was dying, and I wanted to see him again. When I looked into his eyes, I could see the end was nigh and he knew it. Instead of delivering phony words of comfort, I spoke to him in an honest and open manner.

"Dad, I'd like to thank you for everything you've given me in this life. I am capable and powerful, and I will always remember what you taught me. Please move freely. There is nothing to worry about here. I will handle whatever needs to be done.

Tears ran down his face.

"Masako, you are the only one of my children who has actually listened. You never let go of your pride, and you have made me really pleased. I understand how hard you have worked and how much it has cost you, and I'd want to give you something. Open the third drawer of my bureau. Take out the shibori obi. Yes, the one. I made it myself, and it is my favorite. When you discover the man of your dreams, I want you to present it to him."

"I will, Dad, I promise."

I pulled the obi from my father's chest and carried it with me. I saved it till I met my husband. I gave it to him. He still wears it.

My father died three days later, on May 9th. He was seventy-six. I sat near his dead and took his icy hand in mine. I promise you, Dad. I will never forget: Even when starved, the samurai shows no signs of weakness. "Pride comes first."

Even though we have only lived together for a few years. I had always loved my father and kept him dear to my heart. I was devastated by his passing.

Mama Masako gave me some money. I pulled the purple silk wrapping from my obi and handed it to my mother. I didn't know how much it was, but I'm guessing quite a bit.

"I'm not sure whether this is enough, but I want you to give Dad the funeral he would have preferred. If you require any additional supplies, please contact Kuniko or me.

"Oh, Ma-chan, thank you very much. I'll do my best. But not everyone here listens to what I say."

She cast a glance toward the other room. Yaeko's low, sarcastic laugh floated in over the sound of clinking mahjong tiles. I felt horrible, but there wasn't much else I could do.

As an adopted member of the Iwasaki family, I was unable to help my mother in any official capacity. I looked at her with empathy and said, "Mom, I want you to know that I have never stopped loving you or Dad, and I never will. Thank you so much for giving me this life."

I bowed and departed.

When I arrived home, Mama Masako asked me, "Did you give your mother money for the funeral?"

"Yes, I handed her whatever was in the purple silk wrapper."

"Good. It is critical that you learn to spend money properly and to use it at the appropriate moments. It is acceptable to offer gifts of congratulations after the event, but not gifts of bereavement. These should be provided in a timely manner. This is one moment when it is critical not to be stingy; we do not want to lose face. Now, make sure your mother has plenty. If she doesn't, I'll cover the extra costs.

This was quite generous of her. And I was relieved mom was finally teaching me how to handle money properly. But, when you think about it, the money she gave me to give to my mother was money I made on my own.

Another significant event in 1973 was receiving accreditation (natori) from the Inoue School, which recognized me as a master dancer. The biggest advantage of being a natori is that you can now learn and execute roles that were previously restricted for master dancers. That autumn, I was cast as Princess Tachibana in the Onshukai.

Big Mistress stood with me behind the curtain as I was about to enter the hanamichi, the elevated walkway that connects the back of the theater to the stage. She bent down and whispered into my ear. "All I can do is teach you the form. "The dance you perform on stage is yours alone."

The broadcast was completed. I was free. The dance was mine.

However, simply being certified did not grant me the right to teach. Only teachers who had been taught in this manner since the beginning were permitted to do so. It did not imply that I could perform outside of the carefully restricted environment of the Inoue School or the Kabukai. I still had to follow their regulations. So, while it was beneficial to my job, the qualification was practically meaningless. It did not help to achieve professional or financial independence.

In midsummer, Kyoto commemorates Obon (All Souls' Day) by lighting a massive bonfire on a mountainside to guide our ancestors' souls back to their faraway abodes. The fire is visible from anywhere in the city.

In Gion Kobu, black lacquer pans are filled with water and placed on the verandahs of the ochaya to capture the reflection of the flames.

Attendees at the ozashiki that evening take a taste of the water from the platter and pray for health. This casual ritual marks the start of the summer vacation.

I used to spend a few weeks in August at Karuizawa, Japan's premier summer resort. I did not consider this a vacation. It was more of a business trip. Many government and corporate executives have country homes in Karuizawa, as does the aristocracy, which has long sought refuge in this mountain hideaway during the humid summer months. In the 1950s, Japan's current emperor, Akihito, met Empress Michiko on a tennis court in the city center.

I spent my evenings traveling from one house to another, entertaining the power brokers and their guests. Sometimes I would run into Big Mistress while she was making her own rounds. She was a different person when she was in the country, gentler and less solemn. She would sit down, and we would converse.

She described what it was like throughout the conflict. "There was very little food. We were all famished. I moved from place to place, laid out a mat on the floor, and danced. People handed me rice and vegetables. This is how I fed my students. It was a difficult existence. "I thought it would never end."

I enjoyed hearing her stories. I saw glimpses of the spirit she must have possessed when she was younger.

Karuizawa's mornings were all mine, and I relished the tranquility. I woke up at six a.m. and went for long morning walks. Then I read until it was time to meet Tanigawa Sensei at the Akaneya Café at ten o'clock. Dr. Tanigawa and I spent many valuable hours together during those long summer days. I was able to ask him whatever I wanted. He never tired of offering me well-thought-out responses.

He enjoyed a nice cup of coffee and would get a new flavor every day. Instant geography lesson. He would enjoy telling me about the part of the world where the coffee came from. One thing led to another, and before we knew it, it was lunchtime. There was a soba restaurant across the street from the cafe. We ate there frequently.

Many of my friends visited Karuizawa at the same time that I did. The majority of them traveled by bicycle, but I didn't know how to ride. I was too embarrassed to admit it, so I wandered about pushing a bicycle's handlebars. I'm not sure who I thought I was kidding.

One day, I ran into someone I knew.

"Hi there, Mineko. How are you? "And what are you doing?"

"What do you think I'm doing?" "I am pushing this bike."

"Really? Just think: I always assumed bicycles were something you sat on and pedaled. I never realized you were supposed to push them."

"That's very humorous. If I knew how to ride it, I would.

"You mean you can't ride?"

"Obviously not."

"Then why don't you ride about in a horse carriage?"

"Wouldn't that be lovely!"

"Come with me then. "My treat."

She drove me to a nearby hotel and booked a horse carriage. I parked my bicycle in the driveway and spent the afternoon cycling around by myself. I must admit, I felt like royalty. I was having a great time.

CHAPTER 13
SHATTERED LOVE

For five years, I believed that Toshio would divorce his wife and marry me. During this time, he lied to me twice. Both lies concerned his family. The first time he told me he had to leave town for work, he was actually spending the night in Kyoto with his wife, who had traveled down from Tokyo to see him. The second occurred as we were returning to Tokyo from San Francisco. He told us we had to disembark the plane individually because he had heard there were media at the gate. I dutifully complied, always wanting to avoid scandal. There were no reporters. When I exited customs, I noticed his wife and children had arrived at the airport to greet him home.

I know I said at the start of our relationship that lying was unacceptable, but life isn't that simple. Once we were involved, I realized I wanted to give Toshio time to think it all out before taking the ultimate step.

But after five years, I understood he wasn't buying it, and I had to face reality. We were no closer to being a true relationship now than we had been that night at the Waldorf. I decided to terminate the relationship and start seeking for the proper opportunity. He was generous enough to give it to me.

In March 1976, Toshio lied to me for the third and final time.

I used to travel frequently to Tokyo for business. When I was alone, I remained on the women's floor of the New Otani Hotel; however, when I was with Toshio, we always stayed in the same suite on the fifth level of the Tokyo Prince Hotel. I can still recall the number of our rooms.

We had planned to meet in Tokyo one evening, so when I arrived, I booked into our suite. I was organizing my makeup and toiletries on the bathroom vanity when the phone rang. It was Toshio.

"I am in the middle of a production meeting. It appears that this will last for several hours. Would you mind making alternative plans for dinner? "I'll catch you later."

I contacted a dear friend who lives nearby. She was free for dinner. After eating, we decided to head out and have some fun. We visited all of Roppongi's hot spots and discos. It had been a long time since I let go, and I had a terrific time.

I arrived back at the motel around three o'clock in the morning. When I stepped in, one of Toshio's attendants was seated in the foyer and rushed up to greet me.

"Are you waiting for me?" I asked.

"Yes, Miss, I…"

"Is Toshio all right?"

'Yes, he is fine. But he's still attending a meeting. He handed me the key and instructed me to accompany you safely to your room.

This didn't make much sense to me, but I was too weary to worry.

We walked into the elevator, and he pressed the button for the eighth level.

"I apologize, but that's the incorrect floor. "I'm staying at five."

"No, I do not believe that. "I was told you're staying at eight."

This is quite strange, I thought as Toshio's aide unlocked the door to a chamber I'd never seen before. It was not a suite. I turned to speak to the assistant, but he was quickly bowing his way out of the room. He said evening and closed the door behind him.

I looked around. My bags were precisely where I left them. My toiletries were set up in the same order on the vanity. I felt as if I'd fallen into the hands of a genie. I took a bath and went to bed, too exhausted to think about what was going on.

Toshio called at 4 a.m. "The meeting should be over in a while, but I'm still here."

In other words, I won't be seeing him anytime soon.

"Why did the room change?"

"Oh, well, you know what, I'll tell you about that later. "There are people present now..."

He made it sound as if he couldn't speak in front of others. But it did not ring true. It sounded like he was hiding something. The next morning, I decided to investigate what was going on. I explained to the man at the front desk, who knew me, that I had misplaced my key. He asked a bellboy to take me to the suite and open the door.

There was no one in the room, but plainly someone had been. The bed was untidy. There were used towels on the bathroom floor. I opened the closet. There was a fur coat hanging and a woman's purse on the floor. Needless to say, these were not mine.

Because this was supposed to be my room, I had no reservations about opening the bag. I looked inside, and among the garments was a stack of headshots of Toshio's wife. The photos were the kind one autographs for fans. Toshio must have had my belongings moved sometime after I left last night so that his wife could move in. I exploded. How could he? I didn't really care if she was his wife. It was our room! And I'd been there first.

I later learned that Toshio and his wife had to make a last-minute appearance on a television show together. But nonetheless, when he found out she was coming, he should have rented another room rather than having my belongings shifted from one room to another.

I trembled at the thought of what this implied. This was the truth. His wife arrived first. She was more valuable to him than I was. Why else would he have gone to such lengths? If he had only told me his wife was coming, I would have checked out and gone to the New Otani hotel. I would not have checked into a room on the eighth story of the Prince, where I had a decent possibility of running into her.

It was just too much. I contacted housekeeping and requested a huge set of shears. I tore the fur coat off its hanger. I took the scissors and ripped it into small pieces. Then I flipped her bag upside down and dumped it on the bed. I threw her photographs all over the pile and shoved the scissors into the center.

Okay, Toshio. You've made your decision. Now deal with it. Sayonara.

I went up to my eighth-floor room, packed my luggage, and exited through the lobby. I promised to never return to that suite or hotel again. Toshio had no reaction to what I'd done. He continued to treat me as if nothing had happened, without discussing the event.

I anticipated him to confront me about my wanton behavior. In my fantasies, I made amends for the coat and declared independence. His hesitation to bring it up put us in a strange holding pattern. I began preparing myself to terminate it completely.

Toshio invited me to join him on a family excursion to the Yugawara hot springs resort. We went with his parents, his brother (a well-known actor), and his brother's girlfriend, an actress. It was not unusual that I was traveling with this artistically skilled company. His parents appreciated the cachet that I brought to the gathering as a geiko and welcomed me into their circle. They approved of my relationship with their son, and we got along well.

The resort had prepared a seasonal "iris bath," a traditional spring tonic to refresh the body and soul. Seeking seclusion, I stepped into the bath alone and pondered what to do. What to say? How to exit the situation graciously. I eventually made a decision. I'd say nothing. I would end it simply by no longer being available.

Toshio loved driving. He owned a gold Lincoln Continental and a hunter green Jaguar and drove quite quickly. The next morning, he drove me back to Tokyo and dropped me off at the inn where I was supposed to stay. As soon as he was out of sight, I grabbed a taxi and headed to New Otani. Toshio suspected something was wrong. He circled the street and returned to locate me. But I was gone.

I checked into the motel and threw myself onto the bed. I laid there alone for hours, weeping my eyes out. I was still attempting to rationalize the relationship: why can't I just leave things as they are? What difference does it make if he is married? But the truth is, it did matter. I refused to remain second best any longer.

When I couldn't cry anymore, I called a close friend. I was so popular at the time that I could go into sumo matches for free. They say, "My face was my ticket." I invited a friend to join me that evening. She was not busy and agreed to go.

We were situated in the first row "sand spray" seats, so named because they collect the sand flung off the stage by the wrestlers. We'd hardly settled in when the man himself walked in. I became agitated and quickly exited. I couldn't bear to be around him. I came home to Kyoto and, following correct etiquette, called the okasan of the ochaya who was acting as our go-between to advise her of our separation.

Toshio refused to let the issue go. He asked to see me, but I declined. His mother also joined in. She came to the okiya several times to speak with Mama Masako and me. She begged me to reconsider. "He is heartbroken over this, Mineko. Could you kindly alter your mind? The more she pleaded, the more confident I felt that I had done the correct thing.

Finally, they gave up, and it was over. So this is how it ended. This is how I destroyed the love of my life. In my heart, "Toshio" had died. He became known simply as Shintaro Katsu, the actor. Now that I was on my own, I started thinking about gaining true freedom.

I was so fed up with the system. I had followed the rules for years, but there was no way I could remain in the system and do what I wanted. The primary reason for Gion Kobu's systematization was to ensure the dignity and financial independence of the women who worked there. However, the Inoue School's strictures held us under its power. There was no room for any form of autonomy.

We are not only not allowed to teach, but we are also not allowed to perform whenever and wherever we want. We must obtain permission for everything, from our choice of repertoire to the accessories and props we may utilize. This arcane system has remained untouched for almost a century. It contains no procedure for change, improvement, or reform. Complaining or resisting is unacceptable. As previously stated, I had attempted to make systemic changes since the age of fifteen. To no avail.

Another important issue is that we performers get paid very little for our public performances, including the Miyako Odori, despite its popularity and capacity crowds. A small few (the teachers) are said to profit handsomely from the operation, while those of us who really perform on stage receive very little. This comes after we spent a month rehearsing and selling tickets. (We sell tickets as part of our job. I frequently asked my best customers to purchase large quantities of them as employee and client giveaways. I used to sell 2,500 each season.

So while we support the dance, it does not support us. And we are not mountaintop sages who can survive on consuming mist.

I was now twenty-six and responsible for the okoya's continuation. I began to appreciate the strain Auntie Oima had been under when she discovered me. I did not want to do it. Because of my status, I was besieged by younger maiko who wanted me to become their official Onesan. I explained that while the Nyokoba school is recognized by the Ministry of Education as a specialist school, it does not provide high school diplomas. Regardless of how hard you work, you will wind up where you started: with a junior high school education. You will not have the necessary academic credentials or certifications to function in the real world. Even if you do exceptionally well and obtain a master's credential from the Inoue School, you will be unable to sustain yourself. I've been trying to improve things for years, but no one has listened. So, I apologize, but as long as things continue as they are, I do not feel safe taking on any younger sisters. However, if you'd like, I may connect you to another geiko who may be prepared to sponsor you."

Without younger sisters, the okiya's company could not develop. The geiko with us was getting older. Revenues were down. I didn't want to ask any of my customers for more business, even if several volunteered. I had no desire to incur that amount of debt or duty since it would conflict with the concept of the independent businesswoman instilled in me by all of my mentors. My alternatives were restricted. I needed to find another means to make money.

Around that time, a friend of mine, who worked full-time as a geiko, started her own nightclub on the side. There was little precedent for this type of dual role in the Gion, and her unconventional behavior was strongly discouraged, but I thought it was fantastic.

I resolved to do the same thing myself. I'd renovate the okiya and convert part of it into a nightclub! Once the club was established, I could utilize the cash to support my family and do whatever I pleased. Mama Masako could assist me in the club when I needed her.

But I was in for a major surprise. It turned out that we did not own the okiya! Unbeknownst to me, we had been renting it for years. We couldn't renovate something we didn't own. I tried to persuade Mama Masako to buy the house, but my reasoning went unheeded. Her response to our difficulties was to hoard money rather than spend it. She had no notion of investing for the future. She felt renting was okay.

I did not. I went behind her back. I called the bank and, based on my wages, was able to obtain a mortgage and purchase the property with my own funds. But then I hit another roadblock. The house was over a century old and so legally ineligible for refurbishment. Ordinance mandated that we had to dismantle it and start again. I was prepared to proceed, but Mama Masako was utterly opposed to the notion.

I was determined not to give in. My load was excessively heavy. Each year, I participated in eleven different performing programs. I enjoyed the dancing, but it wasn't enough to support the okiya. The only way I could supplement my family's income was to increase the number of ozashiki I worked, but I was already overburdened.

I still planned to build a new building on the site of the okiya, but I recognized it would take some time to persuade Mama Masako to support my plans. But, as usual, I could not wait. So I went out, found a place to rent, and found investors eager to invest in a club.

In June 1977, I opened my own place. I dubbed it Club Hollyhock. When I was not present, my partner oversaw the operation. But every afternoon, before I went to work, I checked that everything was in order. And every night, once I finished my ozashiki, I went to the club and stayed until it closed.

CHAPTER 14
A BOLD STEP TOWARD CHANGE

Over the next three years, I steered a steady course toward retirement. The nightclub was simply a temporary solution. My true ambition was to start a business that made women more beautiful. I wanted to run a beauty treatment facility, and I devised a plan to make it happen.

First, I needed a place. I had to persuade Mama Masako to allow me to construct a building. I believed it should be five stories. I would build the club on the first story, a beauty treatment clinic and hair shop on the second, and divide the above floors between our living quarters and rental renters. This should provide me with adequate revenue to support the household.

Next, I had to decide what would happen to all of the geiko and staff under the okoya's care. I would negotiate engagements for ladies who wished to marry, and assist others in finding new jobs or starting their own businesses.

Then I could choose how and when to retire. The press claimed that I was the most successful geiko in a hundred years. I wanted to use this momentum for good. My retirement would deal a significant damage to the system. I hoped that the shock of my defection and its consequences would serve as a wake-up call to the conservative leadership, forcing them to rethink their ways. I wanted them to see that the Gion Kobu's organization was dangerously out of step with the times, and that unless they implemented reforms, the Gion Kobu would be doomed.

From where I stood, the karyukai's demise seems imminent. The organization was so inactive that it was strangling the very treasures it was supposed to protect. The truth is that, even at the time, the number of okiya and ochaya in Gion Kobu was decreasing. The proprietors of the ochaya and okiya were primarily concerned with immediate profit; they lacked a shared vision for the future.

I couldn't sit by and let Gion Kobu vanish into oblivion. Maybe I still had time to make a difference. I made a daring decision. I would retire before I hit thirty. I resolved to aggressively seek ways to supplement my income.

Keizo Saji, Suntory's president, called me around that time.

"Mineko, we're going to film a commercial for Suntory Old, and I was wondering if you could advise the maiko on their movements? Could you meet me at the Kyoya Moto restaurant at four tomorrow afternoon?

Mr. Saji was an excellent customer, and I was delighted to oblige.

I wore a light blue early summer silk crepe kimono with a white heron pattern and a five-color obi embossed with a gold watermark pattern.

When I arrived, two maiko were preparing for the shoot, which was scheduled for one of the traditional-style restaurant's private tatami rooms. A modest table near the window included a bottle of Suntory Old Whiskey, a bucket of ice, a bottle of mineral water, an old-fashioned glass, a highball glass, and a swizzle stick. I demonstrated the appropriate technique to mix a cocktail to the younger women step by step, and they repeated everything I did. The director asked if I'd mind filming a test.

He had me go along the restaurant's lengthy corridor, decreasing my pace for the camera. The sun was setting in the west, and Yasaka Pagoda glowed on the horizon. We shot this scenario several times before they requested me to open the fusuma into the private chamber. They timed it exactly, such that the Chionin Temple bell rang out a thunderous gong just as I was sliding open the panel.

I sat down at the table and started preparing a drink. I jokingly asked one of the performers, "Would you like it a little stronger?" When the test ended and they began filming for real, I excused myself and went.

Some days later, I was in my room, getting ready for the evening. The TV was on. I heard the sound of a gong and the words, "Would you like it a little stronger?" I had heard that somewhere before, but I wasn't paying attention.

Later that night, I entered an ozashiki, and one of my customers commented, "I see you've changed your tune."

"About what?"

"About being in commercials."

"No, I have not. Mr. Saji did, however, ask me to give some guidance to one of his models. "It was fun."

"I think he pulled a fast one on you."

So it was me, after all!

That old coot made me laugh. I have been duped! I found it weird that he bothered to come to the shoot...

But it was painless, so I didn't mind. "Would you like it a little stronger?" became the buzzword of the day. And the overall experience was accidentally liberating. I figured it wouldn't harm to accept commercial offers and began appearing in pictures, TV commercials, advertising, publications, and talk shows. I was grateful for the extra money and took advantage of any opportunity to discuss the geiko system.

I added advertising work to my already hectic schedule and remained on this treadmill until March 18, 1980, when Mother Sakaguchi died. Her death was a watershed moment in my life. It felt as if the brightest light in Gion Kobu had gone out. Unfortunately, she was the final master of the musical tradition in which she had been schooled. The shape died alongside her.

With Mother Sakaguchi gone, I absolutely lost hope. Any enthusiasm I had for the Gion Kobu lifestyle had vanished. My body was already fatigued. Now my intellect has caught up. Mother Sakaguchi left me an exquisite chalcedony and onyx obi clasp. Whenever I looked at it, I felt not only sad but also desolate, as if my staunchest ally had vanished and left me alone.

Four months later, on July 23, I invited Suehiroya to accompany me on a ceremonial visit to the iemoto. When we entered the studio, Iemoto was on stage by herself. She ended her dance and sat facing us. I placed my fan formally in front of myself.

"I have decided to retire from active service as a geiko on July 25," I told you.

Big Mistress started to cry.

"Mine-chan, I've reared you as my own daughter. I've seen you go through so much, from diseases to accomplishments. Would you please reconsider your decision?"

A thousand memories rushed through my mind: her coaching, rehearsing, and granting me permission to perform this or that piece in public. I was struck by her emotion, but she couldn't express what I really wanted to hear. She couldn't say, "Whatever you do, Mineko, please don't stop dancing." The system would not allow it. When I quit being a geiko, I also had to stop dancing.

My mind was made up. I bowed to Big Mistress and delivered my final declaration in a firm voice. "I am grateful for the many years of compassion you have shown me. I will never forget the amount I owe you. "My heart is full of gratitude."

I pressed my forehead against the floor. The dresser remained speechless. I went home to tell Mama Masako and Kuniko. They both burst into tears. I advised them to pull themselves together because there was so much to do in the following 48 hours. We needed to make goodbye gifts for everyone in the neighborhood.

Big Mistress must have alerted the Kabukai right away, because the phone rang nonstop for the next two days. Everyone wanted to know what was going on. The officers of the Kabukai wanted clarification. They implored me not to resign. However, they did not offer to make any changes.

That night, I attended my scheduled ozashiki. I pretended that nothing remarkable was happening. Everyone inquired what was wrong and why I was going. I only said, "Well, these fifteen years may have seemed short to you but they have been an eternity for me."

It was well past midnight by the time I arrived at the Hollyhock. The place was packed. I was instantly overwhelmed with exhaustion. I took the microphone and declared my retirement from the profession. Saying it out loud made it feel more genuine. I requested everyone to leave and then closed the place a couple hours early.

I arrived at Nyokoba around 8:20 the next morning for my class. Big Mistress and I worked on the dance Yashima Island, which can only be mastered by individuals who have gained certification. The lecture lasted much longer than normal. When I stepped off the stage, she looked me in the eye and let out a large sigh.

There was nothing more to say.

I drew into myself and bowed deeply. This was it, I thought. There's no turning back now. It is over.

I took a second dancing lesson with one of the small mistresses, as was my custom, followed by a Noh dance class and a tea ceremony class. I paid my respects to my teachers, bowed goodbye in the genkan, and walked out the Nyokoba door for the final time. I was twenty-nine years and eight months old, and my time as a geiko in Gion Kobu had come to an end.

As expected, my retirement caused shockwaves through the system. But not in the way I had intended. Seventy other geikos left the business within three months of my retirement. I appreciated the gesture, even though it seemed a little late to express unity with me at the time. The powers that be made no changes.

CHAPTER 15
THE STORY CONTINUES

I woke up on July 25 feeling as free as a bird. I stretched out luxuriously in my bed and took up a book. I didn't have to attend class. The other women in the house were well taken care of. I just had to care about my "real" dependents, Kuniko and Mama.

Kuniko's dream was to open a restaurant. I vowed to carry her for three years, and she was busy preparing her new business. If the business was successful, she may continue; if it failed, we would shut it down. She named the restaurant Ofukuro no Aji, which translates to Mother's Home Cooking.

Mama Masako was the only one who wasn't preparing to go out on her own. I had calmly explained my plans to her several times, but she still didn't understand. She was used to relying on others and had no drive to establish a life for herself. She mostly liked things the way they were. What was I supposed to do? I couldn't kick her out. When I stood alongside her in court and declared, "I want to be adopted by the Iwasaki family," I accepted a significant responsibility. I felt compelled to look after her.

Mama Masako and I had slightly different perspectives on what it meant to be an atotori. I took my duty to Auntie Oima to mean that I was obligated to carry on the Iwasaki name and retain its artistic integrity. I did not interpret this as a vow to handle the okiya indefinitely. Mama Masako wanted the okiya to continue.

"Mine-chan, you're not growing any younger. Have you started thinking about who will be your atotori?

It was time to be honest with her. I stated clearly: "Please understand, Mama." I don't want to manage the okiya. I am tired of this industry and want to leave. If it were up to me, I'd close the okiya tomorrow. But there is another possibility. If you wish to keep it going, I will relinquish my position and you can find someone else to be the atotori. I will give you whatever is in my savings account. "You and your next heir can run the okiya, and I'll return to being a Tanaka."

"What are you talking about?" You're my daughter. How could I possibly replace you? If you wish to close the okiya, we'll close it."

It wasn't what I had hoped she would say. I was half hoping she'd accept my offer and relieve me of my responsibilities to her and the okiya. But life is never so simple.

Okay, Mama. I understand. So let's strike a deal. You are invited to remain with me, with one condition. I want you to promise not to interfere with my plans. Even if you believe I am making a mistake, I need you to allow me to do things my way. "If you promise, I will care for you for the rest of your life."

She consented and ultimately gave me permission to demolish the okiya and develop my dream for the future. I didn't feel guilty about closing the okiya. I had given the Gion Kobu everything I had, and it was no longer meeting my needs. I didn't have any regrets.

I purchased a huge apartment, and we lived there while the new building was being constructed. I wrapped up all of the okiya's lovely costumes and artifacts and put them safely in my new home. The building was finished on October 15, 1980. Due to Mama Masako's suggestions (read interference), I had to revise my plans, and the building ended up being three floors rather than five. But that was definitely better than nothing.

I opened the new Club Hollyhock on the ground floor. Kuniko opened Mother's Home Cooking. We moved into an apartment on the second floor. I wanted to build a beauty treatment center on the third floor, but in the meanwhile, we used the area for guest accommodations and storage.

I was enjoying the relative simplicity of my new life. On a dare from several of my customers, I took up golf. After a few weeks of private sessions, I was consistently scoring in the 80s and 90s. Nobody believed me, but I believe that golf, like basketball, came naturally to me because dancing had improved my balance and given me an uncommon level of fine motor control.

I began to conduct extensive research on the beauty industry and construct a beauty therapy facility. I tested various items and interacted with a wide range of specialists in the subject. One of my customers volunteered to refer me to a skilled hairdresser in Tokyo who could be of assistance. My customer's wife arranged the meeting and agreed to make the introduction. When I got in town, I called Mrs. S. to finalize our plans. She invited me to stop by for a conversation if I wasn't too busy, and with some free time, I decided to take advantage of her hospitality. Mrs. S. cordially greeted me and led me into the living area. There on the wall was the most incredible painting I'd ever seen. It was a stunning shot of a nine-tailed fox.

"Who painted that picture?" I inquired, buzzing with the sense that something significant was going on.

"Isn't it a beautiful painting? We're keeping it here for the artist. His name is Jinichiro Sato. I am studying with him. His career is just getting started, but I believe he is extremely brilliant."

I was shaken by a sudden insight. I am intended to showcase this artist to the world. I knew this was what I was destined to accomplish. It seemed as if someone had assigned me a mission.

I asked my Mrs. S. a lot of questions about the painting, and then it was time for me to meet Toshio for supper. Over the last few years, we've salvaged a friendship from the ruins of our love. Mrs. S. and I were not scheduled to meet with the hairdresser until later that evening.

"I'll see you at the Pub Cardinal in Roppongi at ten-thirty," I remarked, thanking her for her kindness and departing.

Toshio and I had a great supper, and then he took me to his office. He sought my feedback on something he was working on. We watched and discussed the footage. Then he insisted on taking me to Roppongi by himself. I was a couple of minutes late. I noticed someone who I believed may be Mrs. S. (like Kuniko, I am nearsighted), but the woman was sitting with two people rather than one, so I assumed I was mistaken. They all began waving me over, so I grinned my way across the room to them. One of the men was quite young and attractive.

Mrs. S introduced me to the hairdresser. He was not the one. She then turned to the other man. "And this is Jinichiro Sato, the artist whose painting you admired earlier."

"But you're so young!" I said.

"I most certainly am not!" he retorted forcefully. (He was twenty-nine).

"I love that painting," I remarked without hesitation. "Is there any way I could buy it from you?"

"Oh, you can have it," he said. "Take it." It is yours.

I was dumbfounded.

"No, no, I couldn't do that," I responded. "It's far too valuable." Besides, if I don't pay for it, I won't consider it my."

But he will not hear of it. "If you like the painting that much I would really like you to have it." He sounded entirely serious.

Mrs. S agreed with him.

"Be gracious, my dear, and take advantage of his kind offer."

"Well, in that case, I accept the painting gratefully and will return the favor to you somehow in the future."

I had no clue how prophetic those statements would prove to be. Meanwhile, I spent so little time speaking with the hairdresser that we had to reschedule our appointment for the following evening.

I saw Jin a few more times during the next few weeks. He always seemed to show up when I met Mrs. S. Then I was invited to a house party at their place in early November, and he was there. He stared at me for a long time, but I didn't notice. He was extremely sharp. Very funny.

On November 6, Mrs. S. called me. "Mineko-san, I'd like to discuss something essential with you. Mr Sato has asked me to speak on his behalf. "He wants to marry you.

I believed she was joking and responded sarcastically. However, she insisted that he was sincere. "In that case," I instructed her, "please tell him no. I will not even consider it."

She began calling me every morning at precisely ten o'clock to reiterate his request. It was becoming bothersome. Apparently, she was doing the same thing to him! She was a brilliant woman. Jin finally called and yelled for me to leave him alone. I yelled back at him that this was none of my doing, and we eventually figured out what Mrs. S. was up to. We both felt humiliated. Jin asked if he may come see me and apologize.

Rather than apologize, he proposed. I refused. He wouldn't accept no as an answer. He returned a few days later. He brought Mrs. S. with him. He proposed again. I refused. I must admit that his cocky assurance piqued my interest. My refusals did not appear to phase him. He arrived again. He proposed again.

Despite myself, I began to think about it. I hardly knew the man, yet he possessed the attributes I was seeking for. I was looking for a means to maintain the refined visual brilliance of the Iwasaki name alive. Introducing a talented artist into the family was one method to accomplish this. And Jin was a fantastic painter. I had no doubts about that. I thought then, as I do now, that Jin would one day be recognized as a National Living Treasure. Not only was he talented. He held a master's degree in art history from Japan's top art school, Tokyo's Geidai, and extensive understanding of the subject.

I wasn't getting younger. I wanted to have kids. I wanted to see what it was like to marry. Jin was also quite likable. There was nothing offensive about him.

I decided to start all over again.

The fourth time he proposed, I agreed on one condition. I made him vow to divorce me in three months if I wasn't satisfied.

We were married on December 2, twenty-three days after meeting.

Because I was to become the head of the household, Mama Masako adopted Jin and gave him the name Iwasaki.

I applied for and acquired a license as an art dealer. I chatted with my supporters at the club and stated my intentions. Everyone offered me their blessing. Mama Masako reacted remarkably calmly. It didn't hurt that Jin was so charming and attractive. Mama quickly established a deep affection for him that she would cherish forever.

I never opened that beauty spa. My carefully laid-out plan vanished as soon as I saw Jin's artwork, and another one appeared. That one painting completely altered my future.

I sold the new building. I closed the club. Jin and I moved into a house in Yamashina. I became pregnant.

Mama continued to reside in Gion Kobu and work as a geiko. Kuniko was a bad entrepreneur who had failed to make the restaurant profitable. She graciously accepted the change of circumstances and moved in with me. She was really excited about the baby's birth.

My adorable daughter, Kosuke, was born in September. Mama continued to work, but she came to see us once a week and was an important part of our family.

Jin is not simply an excellent painter. He is also an expert in art restoration. This component of his work piqued my interest because it required a thorough understanding of art and technique. I asked to study with him, and he accepted me as a student. Kuniko wanted to study as well, so she joined in on the classes after putting the baby to bed. Both of us went on to become certified.

In 1988, we built a large home in Iwakura, a northern suburb of Kyoto, complete with large studios for all of us to work in. My daughter excelled, becoming an elegant and graceful dancer.

I believe this was Kuniko's happiest period in her life. Sadly, she wasn't around long enough to enjoy it. She died in 1996, when she was sixty-three years old.

Mama Masako's eyes started bothering her in the late 1980s, so we decided she should retire. She was in her mid-sixties and had worked hard enough. She, too, enjoyed her retirement years before passing away in 1998 at the age of 75.

At 5:45 a.m. on June 21, 1997, I was awakened by a searing ache in my throat. A little while later, the phone rang.

It was one of Toshio's assistants who called to inform me that he had died early that morning from throat cancer.

Toshio's latter years were not joyful ones. They were dealing with debt, drug issues, and illness.

I attempted to help him in every way I could, but he was dealing with major challenges. Mutual friends advised me not to become involved, and I followed their advice.

Toshio urged me to see him three months before his death. So at least I got the opportunity to say goodbye. Now he was saying goodbye to me.

Yaeko retired two to three years after I did. She sold her Kyoto home and sent the proceeds to her son Mamoru, who built a house in Kobe so she would have somewhere to live. Instead, he spent his wife's money on a house and his mother's money on ladies. When Yaeko came into her new house, she discovered to her dismay that she was not the lady of the manor. Her daughter-in-law gave her a closet-sized room and eventually threw her out.

Yaeko developed Alzheimer's illness in recent years, making her life more difficult than before. Neither my six remaining siblings nor I communicate with her any longer. I am not even sure where she lives. It's a horrible scenario, but I can't help but think she's getting exactly what she deserves.

My days are unconstrained and uncontrolled. I am no longer bound by the rules of the Inoue School. I dance whenever I want. I dance anyway I want. I dance wherever I choose.

I'm thankful for all the blessings and happiness in my life. It's been an unbelievable journey. I am grateful to my father for his pride and honesty in guiding me safely to this serene shore. And thank you, Mother Sakaguchi, Auntie Oima, and Mama Masako, for teaching me to be independent and free.

I am frequently encouraged to return to Gion Kobu. But today I am kindly welcomed as a guest rather than a performance, and I thoroughly enjoy the refined pleasure of attending an ozashiki. I become nostalgic when the youthful maiko and geiko don't recognize me. But they all know who I am. When I tell them my name is Mineko, they always freak out and ask, "Are you the real Mineko?" "The legend?" It's fantastic to spend time with them.

The karyukai is changing. When I retired, there was no shortage of expansive and generous customers who were well-versed in the aesthetic nuances of the trade. Unfortunately, this is no longer the case. It is unclear what the future holds for Japanese society, but it is safe to state that there are fewer truly wealthy individuals than there were in the past, people with the time and resources to maintain the "flower and willow world." I'm concerned the traditional culture of Gion Kobu and the other karyukai may vanish in the near future. The prospect that little of the beautiful tradition will survive beyond its surface appearances saddens me.

The contents of this book may not be copied, reproduced or transmitted without the express written permission of the author or publisher. Under no circumstances will the publisher or author be responsible or liable for any damages, compensation or monetary loss arising from the information contained in this book, whether directly or indirectly. .

Disclaimer Notice:

Although the author and publisher have made every effort to ensure the accuracy and completeness of the content, they do not, however, make any representations or warranties as to the accuracy, completeness, or reliability of the content. , suitability or availability of the information, products, services or related graphics contained in the book for any purpose. Readers are solely responsible for their use of the information contained in this book

Every effort has been made to make this book possible. If any omission or error has occurred unintentionally, the author and publisher will be happy to acknowledge it in upcoming versions.

Copyright © 2024

All rights reserved.

Printed in Dunstable, United Kingdom